Jewish Holiday Cookbook

GREGORIAN CIVIL CALENDAR	HEWBREW CALENDAR AND HOLIDAYS	
SEPTEMBER	TISHRI	ROSH HASHANAH YOM KIPPUR SUCCOT SHEMINI AZERET SIMHAT TORAH
OCTOBER	HESHVAN	
NOVEMBER	KISLEV	HANUKAH
DECEMBER	TEVET	
JANUARY	SHEVAT	TU BISHVAT
FEBRUARY	ADAR	PURIM
MARCH	NISAN	PASSOVER
APRIL	IYAR	YOM HA'AZMAUT LAG B'OMER
MAY	SIVAN	SHAVUOT
JUNE	TAMMUZ	
JULY	AV	TISHA B'AV
AUGUST	ELUL	

Jewish Holiday Cookbook

By Susan Gold Purdy

A HOLIDAY COOKBOOK

FRANKLIN WATTS | NEW YORK | LONDON | TORONTO | 1979

EMPIRE GARDENS

Also by Susan Purdy

CHRISTMAS COOKBOOK
HALLOWEEN COOKBOOK

Library of Congress Cataloging in Publication Data

Purdy, Susan Gold
    Jewish holiday cookbook.

    (A Holiday Cookbook)
    Includes indexes.
    SUMMARY: Presents recipes for traditional
Jewish foods and outlines of the related holidays.
    1. Cookery, Jewish—Juvenile literature. 2.
Fasts and feasts—Judaism—Juvenile literature. [1.
Cookery, Jewish. 2. Fasts and feasts—Judaism. 3.
Holidays]
I. Title
TX724.P8   641.5′67′6   79-4462
ISBN 0-531-02281-1 lib. bdg.
ISBN 0-531-03430-5 pbk.

THIS BOOK IS DEDICATED WITH LOVE
TO MY MOTHER AND MY DAUGHTER AND TO THE
TRADITION OF FAMILIES COOKING TOGETHER

This book is about families sharing the joys of the table. Learning family history while gathering recipes, testing the recipes, cooking together, savoring the results with parents, children, grandparents, sharing the memories (and recipes) of great-grandparents—these are the things that preserve, and create, traditions. To all my family, to aunts, uncles, cousins, and the many friends who contributed their recipes, wisdom, enthusiasm, and time, my grateful thanks.

In particular, I want to thank my husband, Geoffrey, my daughter, Muffin, my sister, Nancy Gold Lieberman, my parents, Harold and Frances Gold, my grandmother, Clara Joslin Schwartz, and my aunts: Bea Joslin, Phoebe Joslin Vernon, Belle Gold, Mildred Gold, and Rosa Queen. Thanks in addition to Lucy Purdy, my mother-in-law; Rhoda Salter, my *mavin*; Maria Peterdi, Marleni Kanas, Mrs. Samuel Katzin, Rachel Katzin Chodorov, Barbara Cover, Julie Glaves, Pat Glaves, Jeanette Sanders, Becky Rossiter, and the late Mrs. Anne Sternberger, Mrs. Bessie Fierstein, Joseph Schwartz, Rebecca Gold, and Harry Joslin.

For carefully reading the manuscript to be sure it was kosher in every sense of the word (though I accept all errors as my own), I thank Mrs. Anne Maidman.

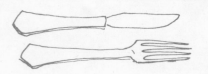 # Contents

Before You Begin

If the arrangement of these recipes looks different to you, it is. In most recipes, ingredients are listed first, then you are told what to do with them. I have told you what foods to get ready in case you are going shopping, then listed ingredients and instructions when and where you actually use them. My testers find this method always works; I hope you will agree. I also hope you will have the patience to read all the way through a recipe before starting it. This will help you plan your time as well as your activities.

If you are kosher, or want to understand the dietary laws, read the chapter on Kosher Cooking (see Contents). This book is designed to be used by kosher as well as non-kosher cooks. All recipes are coded: p (*pareve*) or neutral, D (dairy), M (meat), and Passover, indicating recipes appropriate to each category. Each holiday is introduced by a brief description of its celebration, and the recipes that appear in this book are indicated by *. To find the page, see Contents *or* Index. Each text is followed by a sampling of traditional recipes.

Because they are not noted for special holiday foods, we have taken the liberty of omitting Tisha B'Av (the Holiday of Mourning), and combining Lag B'Omer (the Scholar's Holiday) with Yom Ha'azmaut (Independence Day).

With the help of this book, I hope you will discover the fun of creative cooking, as well as the pride of accomplishment when you make something others enjoy.

1. Safety: Keep pot handles turned away from the stove front so pots will not be bumped into and spilled. Turn off oven or stove-top as soon as you are through using it. When pots are removed from stove, place them on a heat-proof surface. To prevent fires, keep potholders, dishtowels, aprons, and your clothes away from stove burners. Keep a fire extinguisher in the kitchen just in case (and learn how to use it).

To prevent accidental cuts, store and wash knives separately from other utensils.

2. Butter: All butter used for the recipes in this book is lightly salted unless otherwise noted, when the recipe will say "sweet" butter. Margarine can almost always be substituted for butter, and in most recipes both are listed. In recipes that taste much better made with butter, margarine has been left off the ingredients list.

3. Flour: For better nutrition, use *unbleached* all-purpose flour instead of bleached. You will find the word *unbleached* on the front of the flour package. Flour is not sifted unless the recipe specifically calls for it. To sift flour, see Index.

4. Sugar: Sugar is not sifted unless the recipe specifically calls for it. Turbinado (unrefined) sugar can be substituted for an equal amount of granulated white sugar. To substitute honey for granulated sugar, use about ⅞ as much (1 cup sugar = 250 ml = ⅞ cup honey = 220 ml) *and* use about 3 tablespoons (45 ml) *less* liquid in recipe.

5. Eggs: All eggs used in recipes are large size.

6. Wheat germ: To increase nutritional value of recipes, we have added wheat germ wherever possible. We generally prefer to use unflavored toasted wheat germ, but raw unflavored wheat germ may be substituted.

7. Other health-food substitutions: To increase nutritional value of recipes, you can substitute 1 tablespoon (15 ml) sifted soy flour *plus* 1 tablespoon (15 ml) powdered dry milk *plus* 1 tablespoon (15 ml) wheat germ for an equal amount of flour in all cookie and cake recipes. NOTE: Soy flour causes quicker browning, so if you use it, lower oven temperature about 25°.

8. The timer: Whenever a recipe gives two times (such as 10 to 12 minutes), set your timer for the first time (10). Test for doneness. If necessary, reset timer for additional time (2 minutes) and cook longer.

9. Oven heat: Oven temperatures vary. It is very rare for the actual temperature inside the oven to be exactly the same as the one you set on the thermostat dial. If your foods do not cook in the time or manner described in the recipe, it may be because your oven is too hot, or not as hot as the heat indicated by your thermostat. To be safe, use a separate oven thermometer (sold in a hardware store) that hangs or sits on the oven shelf. Change the temperature on your outside thermostat dial until the inside oven temperature is correct.

Kosher Cooking

The word *kosher* literally means "fit," and describes types of food defined by biblical Jewish law as suitable for Jewish people to eat. The origin of these centuries-old laws was not only religious, but also derived from the necessity for preserving food in safe and sanitary conditions in the hot middle-eastern climate without refrigeration.

There are three main categories of kosher foods: Neutral (p) or *pareve* (par'-va), dairy (D) or *milchige* (mil'hig), and meat (M) or *flaishige* (flaish'ig). Neutral (p) dishes are all vegetables, eggs, fruits, and cereals. These may be eaten with both dairy and meat dishes. Kosher fish are also *pareve* (see below). Dairy (D) foods are all milk products, butter, cream, and cheese. Meat (M) dishes must come only from certain "clean" animals (beef and sheep) that have four legs, chew cud, and have cloven hooves. Pigs are forbidden. Acceptable animals must be ritually slaughtered by a *schochet* (sho'hed), or kosher butcher, and then examined. Only perfectly healthy meats may be eaten. All traces of blood must be removed. Some meats are soaked in water and salt to remove all blood. Poultry also must be slaughtered by the *schochet*. Owls, ravens, birds of prey, or scavenger birds are "unclean" and forbidden. Fish with scales and fins are allowed, but shellfish and other seafoods are forbidden. Acceptable fish are considered pareve and can be eaten with either dairy or meat meals. Meat and fish may be served at the same meal if the fish is served first as a separate course on separate dishes. Meat and fish must not be cooked together. Meat and dairy dishes may neither be cooked together nor served together. This law comes from Deuteronomy: "Thou shalt not seethe [cook] a kid in its mother's milk." *Note:* Eggs having a spot of blood are not kosher and may not be eaten.

Originally, kosher cooks used only fats, such as beef or chicken fat, rendered in their kitchens (for directions, see Contents). Now, other fats are allowed. For cooking dairy dishes, one may use butter, margarine (kosher-marked "k"), or vegetable fat or oil. For meat dishes, only kosher margarine (made without milk solids) or vegetable oil (liquid or solid) is permitted, *never* butter. Vegetable fats and oil (liquid or solid) are pareve (p), and may be used anytime. *Note:* Certain brands of kosher margarine may contain milk by-products. Read ingredients before using. Orthodox Jews generally use neither salted butter nor canned milk.

Kosher homes must keep separate sets of utensils, dishes, and pots and pans—one for meat dishes and one for dairy. They are stored in separate cupboards and washed and dried separately. A set of *pareve* dishes, for cooking both meat and dairy dishes, must be made of glass, a nonabsorbent material.

On Passover (see Index for pages with full description), religious laws forbid the eating of any leavened food or *chometz* (ho'-metz). Neither is any leavened food allowed to have touched the dishes or utensils used in the preparation of Passover foods. Thus, another two sets of meat and dairy dishes are kept for Passover use only.

In this book, all recipes are identified by a symbol to indicate their category under kosher law. "Passover" is for Passover use, "p" signifies *pareve,* "D" is dairy, and "M" is meat. If you observe the kosher dietary laws, remember to keep dairy and meat dishes from appearing at the same meal. Sometimes, one can substitute margarine or vegetable oil for butter, or use broth or water instead of milk or cream to convert a dairy dish so as to make it suitable for a meat meal.

Measurements

This book is designed to be used EITHER with standard measurements OR with metric measurements.* In each recipe, you will see both units listed side by side—for example, 1 cup flour (250 ml; 165 g). Select one method and use it consistently. If you choose to cook with the standard method, use the recipes as you ordinarily would, with standard measuring cups and spoons, and ignore the numbers in the parentheses. If you choose the metric system, don't convert, just cook! All the measurements you need are in the parentheses beside each ingredient; ignore the standard cup and spoon measurements. Use metric utensils or the widely available ones with markings in both standard and metric units.

Practical Example   1 cup granulated sugar (250 ml; 210 g)

(select standard cup . . . *or* ml-marked cup . . . *or* weigh on metric scale)

*Irregularities appear in metric measurements because they are rounded off to the nearest useful whole unit.

Basic Skills

To Level Measurements:

All measurements in this book are level unless otherwise specified. To level a measuring cup or spoon, fill it until slightly mounded, then draw the back of a knife blade over the top, scraping the surface flat.

To Measure Butter or Shortening:

Butter or margarine is easiest to measure when purchased in quarter-pound sticks.

1 pound	= 4 sticks	= 2 cups		= 480 ml	= 480 g
1 stick	= ½ cup	= 8 tablespoons		= 120 ml	= 120 g

Instead of measuring by the stick, you can pack the butter down very firmly into a measuring cup (be sure there are no air spaces trapped in the bottom), or you can use the "water displacement" method: To measure ¼ cup (60 ml) butter, fill a 1-cup (250 ml) measuring cup ¾ full (185 ml) with cold water. Add pieces of butter until the water reaches the 1-cup (250 ml) mark. Pour off water and you are left with ¼ cup (60 ml) measured butter.

To Sift Flour:

Sifting lightens the texture of baked goods. You can use either a strainer or a sifter for this process. Flour is sifted only where the recipe specifically calls for it.

Sift the required amount of flour onto a sheet of wax paper. Then pick up the paper, pull the edges around into a sort of funnel, and *gently* pour as much flour as you need back into a measuring cup. You can also use a spoon to transfer flour. Do not shake or pack measured flour. Level top of cup with knife blade, then add flour to recipe. Or return re-measured flour to sifter, add other dry ingredients, such as baking powder and salt, and sift everything together into the other ingredients in recipe.

To Weigh Flour:

Sift flour onto a piece of wax paper as explained above. Then spoon sifted flour lightly onto your wax-paper-lined scale until the measure is correct.

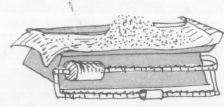

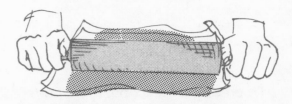

To Roll Out Dough:

There are two ways to roll out dough. One is on a countertop or a pastry board, the other between sheets of wax paper. If you are using a countertop or a pastry board, spread it lightly with flour so the dough will not stick. Also flour the rolling pin. Then roll out the dough, adding more flour if dough sticks. Some pastry boards and rolling pins are covered with cotton cloth (called a sock) to help prevent sticking; cloths should also be floured.

The second method is to cut two pieces of wax paper, each roughly 14″ (36 cm) long. Place one piece flat on the counter and flour it lightly. Place dough on floured paper, then sprinkle a little flour on top of dough. Cover dough with second paper. Use rolling pin (unfloured) to roll out dough between the papers. Peel the paper off and put it back on again if it gets too wrinkled. When dough is correct thickness, peel top paper off dough.

To Separate an Egg:

Here are two different ways to separate an egg. The first method may be new to you, but try it anyway. It is very easy.

First wash your hands, as you will be touching the egg. Crack egg in half by tapping it sharply against side of bowl. Hold egg on its side as shown, grasping ends with your fingers. Fit tips of thumbs into crack. Pull shells apart and *at the same time* turn one half shell upright so it contains all the egg. Hold this shell, containing egg, upright with one hand while the other hand discards the empty half shell. Then turn empty hand palm up, fingers together, over a clean dry bowl. Pour out the entire egg into the fingers of the empty hand. Spread fingers apart very slightly to let the egg white drip between them into the bowl while the yolk rests on top of the fingers as shown. Collect all of the white in a bowl; put yolk in a separate bowl.

The second method is to break egg in half, then hold half shell containing the yolk upright in one hand while you pour the egg white from the other half shell into bowl. Then tip yolk out into the empty shell while white that surrounded it falls into bowl below. Place yolk in separate bowl.

To Use a Garlic Press:

The easiest way to peel the skin off a clove of garlic is to set the clove on a wooden board or counter and smack it hard with the bottom of the garlic press. This breaks the skin so you can pick it off easily with your fingers.

To press the garlic, open the jaws of the garlic press. Set peeled clove inside, then press handles together, forcing garlic out through the holes into the bowl below. Use a spoon or knife to scrape off any pieces of garlic that cling on the outside of the holes. Discard the dry fibers left inside the press. NOTE: If you don't have a press, carefully chop the peeled garlic with a sharp knife.

To Chop an Onion:

"Chopping" with this method means you actually cut the onion into dice, or small pieces. First peel the onion. Then cut the onion in half lengthwise, from root to stem (a). Place one half, cut side down, on board. Hold it with fingers gripping sides, root end to the left (if you are right-handed). Slice onion as shown (b), with point of knife facing root end. Cut almost, but not all the way, through root end; this will help hold onion together. Finally, make narrow cuts in the opposite direction (c), cutting across the first slices to produce the "chopped" or diced pieces. Keep moving your fingers back away from the knife.

To Render Chicken Fat:

Remove the pale yellow lumps of fat from under the skin and inside opening of a chicken's body cavity. Put fat lumps into a saucepan *or* frying pan and set pan on the stove over a low heat. Cook until fat is completely melted (rendered), leaving only small cracklings (*grieben*) that are very good to eat. When rendered, allow fat to cool on a heat-proof surface, then strain and spoon it into a jar for later use in place of butter or margarine.

About Prepared Chicken Fat:

Prepared chicken fat, the consistency of homogenized shortening, is sold in jars in poultry markets, Jewish delicatessens, and supermarkets carrying Jewish products. Good chicken fat should be light yellow-gold in color. Covered and refrigerated, it will keep for a month or longer.

To Make Matzoh Meal:

Crumble whole sheet matzoh over a piece of wax paper. Place about one cup of pieces at a time in a blender container. Turn blender on high and blend until the matzoh is reduced to a fine powder. You can substitute homemade matzoh meal for store-bought, or make more if you run out.

Sabbath

God created the world in six days and rested on the seventh. In the Jewish religion, the Sabbath is observed from sundown on the sixth day, Friday, to sundown on the seventh, Saturday. This is the only holiday mentioned in the Ten Commandments ("Remember the Sabbath Day, to keep it holy"), and thus it is considered one of the most important of all holidays.

Homes are scrubbed and specially prepared to welcome the Sabbath "Queen, or Bride." The best table settings and linens are used for dinner. Two or more white candles are set on the table beside the traditional braided Challah* (ha'-lah). Before dinner, Mother prays as she lights the candles; Father recites the *Kiddush* sanctifying the wine and blesses the bread. The traditional Sabbath meal may include Chopped Chicken Liver,* gefilte fish, Chicken Soup* served with or without Matzoh Balls,* or Borscht,* roasted or baked chicken, Potato Kugel,* and a dessert of fresh fruit, Fruit Compote,* Sponge Cake,* or Apple Kuchen.*

In Orthodox homes, no cooking at all is allowed after the start of the Sabbath, so all dishes are prepared ahead of time. Young people help in all cooking, from the making of the chicken soup to the baking of the challah early on Friday. Some children make their own miniature challah or small twist-shaped buns from the challah dough.

CHALLAH

This challah is the classic Sabbath braided bread traditional in Jewish homes around the world. One recipe will make two full-sized braids or at least eight child-sized braided buns. For Rosh Hashanah, the same dough is baked into round loaves and trimmed with dough ladders and small birds (to help prayers rise to heaven).

EQUIPMENT:
Large mixing bowl and 2 small bowls
Measuring cups and spoons
2-cup measure (500 ml)
Teaspoon
Large mixing spoon
Saucepan
Eggbeater *or* fork
Wooden pastry board *or* washed and dried work surface
Wax paper
Roasting pan *or* pot—optional
Timer
2 cookie sheets *or*, for round Rosh Hashanah loaves, two 3-quart oven-proof bowls
Ruler
Pastry brush
Potholders
Spatula
Wire Rack

FOODS YOU WILL NEED:
2 packages active dry yeast (½ ounce; 14 g) *or* two 1-ounce (28 g) cakes of compressed yeast
3 cups water (750 ml)
4 eggs
½ cup vegetable oil *or* melted margarine (125 ml)
4 teaspoons salt (20 ml)
½ cup granulated sugar (125 ml; 105 g)
7 to 8 cups all-purpose flour (about 1 kg)
⅓ cup poppy seeds *or* sesame seeds (80 ml)—optional

Ingredients:

(To make 2 full-sized loaves or about 8 buns)

¼ cup warm water (60 ml)
2 packages active dry yeast (½ ounce; 14 g) *or* two 1-ounce (28 g) cakes of compressed yeast
2¾ cups warm water (685 ml)
½ cup vegetable oil *or* melted margarine (125 ml)
4 teaspoons salt (20 ml)
½ cup granulated sugar (125 ml; 105 g)
3 eggs

How To:

1. Run ¼ cup (60 ml) water from faucet until comfortably warm, *not hot*, against inside of your wrist. Measure this water into smallest bowl. Sprinkle yeast over water. Stir with teaspoon and set aside.

2. Measure warm (*not hot*) water into largest bowl. Add oil, salt, and sugar. Stir with wooden spoon. One at a time, break eggs into measuring cup, pick out any shells, then add eggs to water mixture in large bowl.

7 to 8 cups all-purpose flour
(about 1 kg)

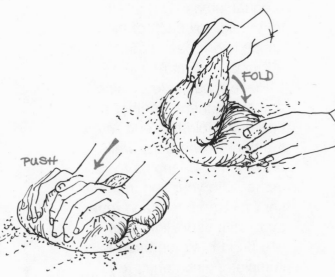

FOLD

PUSH

Beat until eggs are well blended in. When mixture is lukewarm, stir in yeast from step 1.

3. Stir about 1 cup of flour (250 ml) into yeast mixture and beat until well blended. Add another 3 cups flour (750 ml) and beat until dough is blended and begins to look stretchy. Add more flour until dough feels too stiff to stir. Add altogether about 7 cups flour (about 1 kg).

4. NOTE: The exact amount of flour needed will vary, depending upon type of flour and dampness of weather. Sprinkle about ¼ cup (60 ml; 40 g) flour over surface of pastry board or work area. Spoon out all dough onto floured area. Set bowl in sink and fill with warm soapy water to clean it for later use.

5. Sprinkle flour over your hands. Knead dough by folding it over toward you, then pushing it away while leaning on it with the heels of your hands. Give dough a quarter turn and repeat the folding and pushing. The flour from the board will soon work itself into the dough. Add more flour if necessary, and continue kneading about 10 minutes, or until surface of dough looks and feels quite smooth and is no longer sticky to the touch. (If 2 or more people are baking together, they can each knead their own portion of dough.)

6. Wash and dry mixing bowl. Grease inside of bowl with about 1 tablespoon (15 ml) oil. Place ball of dough in greased bowl and roll it upside down so top of dough is oily. This will prevent a dry crust from forming on rising dough. Cover bowl with lightly oiled piece of wax paper.

7. Dough must now rise for the first time. Set bowl in a warm place away from cold drafts. Best rising temperature is between 70° F and 80° F (21° and 27° C); good rising locations are inside your oven (heat *off*!), on the stove-top (heat *off*!), or on a warm corner counter. In cold weather, you can place a pan of warm water on the bottom shelf of the oven beneath rising dough. Dough should rise until double in size; this takes about 1½ hours.

8. To check whether dough has risen enough, poke two fingers into the dough. If holes remain, rising is complete. Then *punch*! your fist right down into the center of the dough. This is fun, and it also knocks some extra air bubbles out of the dough.

PUNCH!

9. Remove dough from bowl and set it onto lightly floured work surface. Knead dough a couple of times to remove some more air. Then grease 2 cookie sheets with a couple of tablespoons of oil (30 ml) and set them aside.

10. Wash hands. Then flour your hands and shape the dough into braids or make round Rosh Hashana loaves as explained.

To shape 2 regular Challah braids, divide the dough in half. Divide each half into 3 equal lumps. To form the first braid, roll each of the 3 lumps into ropes about 1″ × 20″ (2.5 × 51 cm).

Place ropes side by side and pinch them together at one end. Hold this end with the heel of one hand while braiding the 3 lengths together with your fingers as shown. Turn over each rope and pull it very slightly as you braid it. When braid is complete, pinch ends together and tuck pinched ends under loaf. Set braid on greased cookie sheet.

REGULAR BRAID

To make small braided buns, divide dough into 8 equal-sized balls. Then divide each ball into 3 equal-sized lumps. Make braided buns one at a time. First roll 3 lumps into ropes about ¾″ × 7″ *or* 8″ (2 × 20 cm). Set them side by side and braid as described above for large loaf.

NOTE: Leave at least 1″ (2.5 cm) or more space between large or small braids on greased sheet as they grow when they rise and bake.

To make Round Rosh Hashana loaves, divide the dough in half and shape each half into a ball or pat into a thick rope and form a spiral. Place each in a greased round 3-quart baking dish *or* set spirals flat on greased cookie sheet. Leave space between breads on sheet. If you want to decorate round loaves with ladders and birds, first reserve a fist-sized lump of dough before dividing dough in half to form loaves. Model ladder and birds as shown. Dip them into beaten egg glaze (step 12), then set them on top of loaves.

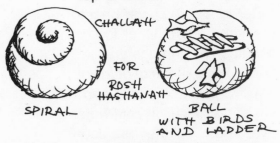

SPIRAL

CHALLAH
FOR
ROSH
HASHANAH

BALL
WITH BIRDS
AND LADDER

11. Cover shaped loaves or buns with lightly greased sheets of wax paper. Again set dough in warm place to rise until *almost* double in size (about 1¼ hours). Do *not* place dough in baking oven for second rising, as oven must be preheated.

SEEDS

12. Turn oven on to 350° F (175° C). To prepare glaze, break remaining egg into a small bowl and beat well. Set egg aside with pastry brush nearby, as well as poppy seeds *or* sesame seeds if you are using them.

13. When dough appears to have grown *nearly* double in size, remove wax paper from top. With a gentle touch, brush beaten egg over tops of loaves. Sprinkle on seeds if using them.

14. Set pans in preheated oven and set timer for 40 to 55 minutes for large braids *or* round loaves, 35 to 40 minutes for buns. Bread is done when it is a rich golden-brown color. Use potholders to remove pans from oven. Tap loaves; they should sound hollow if done. If not quite done, return them to oven for a few mintues more baking. Set pans on heat-proof surface, let bread cool a little, then lift it onto wire racks to cool completely. If loaves stick, lift with spatula. Remove round loaves from bowls as soon as they are baked; cool on wire racks.

Good chopped liver is the Jewish equivalent of a fine French pâté, and this recipe is one of the best! Some cooks claim it can only be made with calves' liver (Mrs. Salter's preference); others prefer chicken livers, which are less expensive but also very good. Try it both ways and decide for yourself. Chopped liver may be served as an hors d'oeuvre, a snack, or as the first course of a dinner.

EQUIPMENT:
Saucepan
Timer
Paring knife and cutting board
Measuring cups and spoons
Frying pan
Small bowl
Strainer—optional
Wax paper
Spoon, fork
Meat grinder *or* blender
Shallow bowl *or* pie plate
Mixing bowl
Serving dish

FOODS YOU WILL NEED:
3 eggs
Water
2 medium-sized yellow onions
About 7 to 8 tablespoons vegetable oil (120 ml) *or* rendered chicken fat (see Index)
1 pound liver (0.5 kg)—calf, beef, *or* chicken
1 whole lemon
Salt and pepper
Parsley—for garnish

Ingredients:

(To make 1½ cups, 375 ml)

3 eggs
cold water

2 medium-sized yellow onions
3 tablespoons vegetable oil (45 ml) *or* rendered chicken fat (see Index)

How To:

1. Set eggs in saucepan and cover them with cold water. Place pan on stove over medium-high heat and bring water to a boil. Lower heat to medium and set timer for 15 minutes. When eggs are done, *ask an adult to help you* remove pan from stove and set it into sink. Run cold water over eggs until they are cool. While eggs are boiling, follow steps 2 and 3.

2. Peel onions. On cutting board cut onions into thin slices. Place oil or fat in frying pan and add onions. Set pan on stove over medium-low heat and cook until onions are golden. When done, remove

1 pound liver (0.5 kg)—calf, beef, *or* chicken

2 tablespoons vegetable oil *or* rendered chicken fat

2 to 3 tablespoons rendered chicken fat *or* oil (30 or 45 ml)

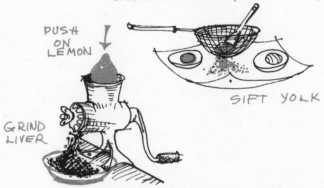

PUSH ON LEMON

GRIND LIVER

SIFT YOLK

pan from heat. Spoon onions into small bowl and set them aside.

3. If using calf or beef liver, cut off any gristle. If using chicken livers, set them, one at a time, on board and slice the two halves apart in the middle. Cut off and discard any yellow fat or discolored areas.

   Place oil or fat in frying pan used for onions. Set pan on stove over medium heat. When oil is warm, add liver and cook it until liver is just done but still slightly pink, *not* well done. This takes 3 to 5 minutes, depending on thickness of liver. Test liver by cutting into it with fork and knife. When done remove pan from heat and let liver cool.

4. Peel eggs. Discard shells. Cut each egg in half. Finely chop (or force through a strainer) one half-yolk; set this aside on wax paper for later use.

   If using meat grinder as shown, place shallow bowl or plate beside grinder to catch food. Use lemon pointy-end-down as a pusher to force food into well. Don't put fingers into grinder! Put cooled liver, onion, and hard-boiled eggs through grinder.

   Or, use blender. BUT, add only a small amount of liver and egg and onion at one time, blending for only 2 *or* 3 seconds. Scoop ground food out into a bowl. Repeat, to blend remaining ingredients. Remember, blending too long will turn liver into a paste.

5. When all ingredients are ground *or* blended and placed in bowl, add 2 *or* 3 table-spoons rendered chicken fat *or* oil (30 or 45 ml)—just enough to hold mixture to-gether, *not* too much, or it will get too oily. Stir in salt and pepper to taste. If you like, add one teaspoon (5 ml) lemon juice for flavor.

6. Mold chopped liver into a ball-shape on a bed of lettuce *or* parsley on serving dish. Decorate top with sprig of parsley *or* sprinkle on re-served egg yolk from step 4. Serve chopped liver spread on crisp crackers.

MOTHER'S CHICKEN SOUP

M

This is IT! Mother's famous chicken soup that cures all illness and tastes good, too. Chicken soup is the traditional first course for Sabbath dinners. The rich golden broth may be served plain *or* with sliced vegetables *or Kreplach* or* Matzoh Balls* in it. As you will cook the vegetables and chicken together, you actually make two dishes at once. The cooked chicken can be placed on a platter surrounded by the cooked carrots for the main course. NOTE: Be sure to ask an adult for help where indicated in this recipe.

EQUIPMENT:
5- or 6-quart soup pot with lid (6-liter size)
Measuring cups and spoons
Long-handled fork, large spoon
Paring knife and cutting board
Colander *or* large strainer
Large and medium-sized mixing bowls
Slotted spoon
Foley food mill *or* blender—optional

FOODS YOU WILL NEED:
5-pound (2 kg) fowl (soup chicken) cut in pieces, plus gizzard, heart, neck, wing tips
3 *or* 4 stalks celery, plus top leaves
1 large yellow onion
1 sprig fresh dill (*or* 1 teaspoon dried [5 ml])
2 sprigs fresh parsley (*or* 1 teaspoon dried [5 ml])
4 *or* 5 quarts water (5 liters)
2 *or* 3 large carrots
Salt, pepper, and paprika

Ingredients:

(To make about 8 servings)

5-pound (2 kg) fowl, cut up, plus gizzard, heart, neck, wing tips
3 *or* 4 stalks celery, plus their leaves (washed well)
1 large yellow onion, skin peeled off
1 sprig fresh dill (*or* 1 teaspoon dried [5 ml])
2 sprigs fresh parsley (*or* 1 teaspoon dried [5 ml])
NOTE: Wrap dill and parsley together in cheesecloth for easy removal from cooked soup.
4 to 5 quarts water (5 liters)

2 *or* 3 large carrots, washed, tips and stems cut off (if very fat, cut carrots in half lengthwise)

How To:

1. Put all fowl parts into large soup pot. Add celery, onion, dill and parsley. Cover all with water. Set pan on stove, cover, and turn on high heat under pot. When water boils, lower heat to simmer chicken about 1½ to 2 hours. *Ask an adult to help you test chicken's doneness.* Chicken is done when thickest parts feel tender when poked with long-handled fork.

2. When chicken is cooked, turn off stove. *Ask an adult to help you add carrots.* (Splashed hot soup may cause burns!)

Turn heat under pot to medium and set timer for 30 to 60 minutes. Simmer soup until carrots are just tender. Then turn off heat.

3. Set colander *or* strainer in large bowl in sink. *Ask an adult to help with this step.* Ask adult to remove pot from stove and set it on heat-proof surface. Use long-handled fork *or* slotted spoon to lift out chicken and vegetables, placing them in medium-sized bowl. Ask adult to pour soup from pot into colander *or* strainer. Bits of chicken and vegetables will be caught and clear broth will be in bowl below. Remove colander *or* strainer from bowl. Discard parsley, dill, onion, and celery leaves. Skim and discard oily fat from top of broth, *or* refrigerate broth until fat is thick and white and easy to lift off in pieces. Taste broth, add salt and pepper as needed for seasoning. Reheat broth to serve.

4. Vegetables may be eaten separately, *or* the carrot and celery stalks may be sliced up and added back to the broth. *Or*, you can put all vegetables through the food mill *or* liquefy them in the blender, then return them to soup. Broth will no longer be clear if you add ground-up vegetables to it, but the flavor is great! Separate chicken from bones and set it on serving platter. Sprinkle chicken with paprika and garnish with fresh parsley. *Or*, cool and make chicken into a salad. *Or,* remove bones, cut chicken into small bits and return it to soup.

PHOEBE'S BEET BORSCHT

Borscht is Russian in origin. There are many variations of this popular soup, some made with meat and vegetables, others with cabbage. Our favorite is non-meat beet borscht, served either hot or cold in a bowl with a spoonful of sour cream and half a boiled potato. (If Kosher, only serve with sour cream for all-dairy meal.) This recipe describes borscht-making from scratch; if you are in a hurry, use canned beets and their juice in place of cooked fresh beets and their liquid in the steps below. NOTE: Be sure to ask an adult for help when noted in the recipe, as spilled hot soup causes burns.

EQUIPMENT:
Vegetable peeler
Paring knife
Large pot *or* Dutch oven with lid
Measuring cups and spoons
Lemon squeezer—optional
Timer
1 medium and 2 small mixing bowls
Long-handled wooden spoon
Wire whisk *or* large spoon
Long-handled fork
Wax paper or cutting board
Blender *or* grater

FOODS YOU WILL NEED:
8 medium-sized beets (about 2¾ pounds; 1 kg)
1 medium yellow onion
1 tablespoon salt (15 ml)
2½ quarts water (2.5 liters)
⅓ cup lemon juice (80 ml) *or* about 1¼ whole lemons
3 tablespoons granulated sugar (45 ml)
1 egg
Sour cream and potatoes, boiled and peeled and cut in half—optional

Ingredients:

(Makes about 2½ quarts soup [2½ liters] or *10 servings of 1 cup each)*

8 medium-sized beets (about 2¾ pounds; 1 kg)
1 medium yellow onion
1 tablespoon salt (15 ml)
2½ quarts water (2.5 liters)

⅓ cup lemon juice (80 ml) *or* 1¼ whole lemons
3 tablespoons granulated sugar (45 ml)

How To:

1. Peel beets with vegetable peeler. Cut off stems and roots. Rinse beets and put in large pot *or* Dutch oven. Peel onion and put it into same pot. Add salt and water, cover pot, and set over high heat. Bring water to boil, then lower heat to medium and set timer to 60 minutes.

2. Squeeze lemon juice into small bowl, remove pits, and place juice in measuring cup. When you have enough juice, return it to small bowl, stir in sugar, and set it aside while beets cook.

1 egg

3. Break egg into second small bowl. Beat with whisk *or* fork. Set egg aside while beets cook.

---

4. After 60 minutes of cooking, test beets for doneness. To do this, *ask an adult to help you.* Turn off heat under pot. Ask adult to poke beets with a long-handled fork; beets should be soft through like a baked potato. When beets are done, ask adult to lift pot off stove and place it on a heat-proof surface. Use long-handled fork to lift out beets and onion and place them in medium-sized mixing bowl.

5. Add lemon juice-sugar mixture to beet liquid left in pot. Allow to cool.

6. Add about 2 cups (500 ml) cool beet liquid from pot to beaten egg. Beat mixture together with whisk while adding liquid so that egg blends instead of cooking. Slowly pour this egg-beet juice mixture back into the large pot. Whisk *or* beat thoroughly until soup is smooth.

7. Set whole beets on wax paper *or* cutting board. Cut beets into quarters with paring knife.

Set out blender *or* grater. If using blender, put about 8 quarter-pieces at a time into container along with about ½ cup (125 ml) beet soup from pot. Blend 4 *or* 5 seconds, until beets are chopped but

not liquefied. Remove container from motor and add chopped beets to soup in pot. Repeat until all beets are blended.

If using grater, use either the smallest *or* the medium-sized holes of the grater. Grate all beets over a piece of wax paper. Add grated beets to soup in pot.

Onion may be blended *or* grated and added to soup *or* just discarded.

8. Stir soup with wooden spoon to blend beets with liquid. Taste and correct seasoning. It should have a strong balanced sweet-sour flavor. Add a little more lemon juice to make it more sour, *or* sugar to sweeten it, if necessary. Chill soup until ready to serve. We prefer to serve it cold, in a bowl over a boiled half-potato, topped by a spoonful of sour cream. (Omit sour cream for meat meal). Borscht is also good hot, and leftovers may be frozen.

MILDRED'S POTATO KUGEL

p

This potato pudding is traditionally served on the Sabbath as an accompaniment to roasted or baked chicken.

EQUIPMENT:
1½ quart (1.5 liter) baking dish
Measuring cups and spoons
Small pot *or* frying pan
Vegetable peeler
Grater
Wax paper
Strainer
Large and medium-sized mixing bowls
Wire whisk *or* eggbeater
Large mixing spoon
Timer
Potholders

FOODS YOU WILL NEED:
5 tablespoons margarine (75 ml)
4 medium-sized white potatoes
3 eggs
½ large yellow onion
1½ teaspoons salt (8 ml)
⅛ teaspoon pepper (0.5 ml)
½ teaspoon baking powder (2.5 ml)
⅓ cup potato starch (60 ml; 55 g)

Ingredients:

(To make 6 to 8 servings)

5 tablespoons margarine (75 ml)

4 medium-sized white potatoes

How To:

1. Turn oven on to 350° F (175° C). Grease baking dish with about 1 tablespoon (15 ml) margarine. Measure remaining margarine into small pot *or* frying pan and set it on stove over low heat to melt. When melted turn off heat.

2. Wash and peel potatoes. Set grater over a piece of wax paper. Grate potatoes on medium-small holes. *Keep fingers well back from grater holes!* Use knife to chop last little piece of each potato instead of risking scraped knuckles. Spoon grated potatoes into measuring cup.

(26)

3 eggs

½ large yellow onion

1½ teaspoons salt (8 ml)
⅛ teaspoon pepper (0.5 ml)
½ teaspoon baking powder (2.5 ml)
⅓ cup potato starch (60 ml; 55 g)

You should have about 3 cups (750 ml). Set strainer over medium bowl, then add grated potatoes to strainer and let their water drain out.

3. One at a time, break eggs into a measuring cup, pick out any shell bits, then add eggs to large bowl. Beat eggs with whisk *or* beater.

4. Cut another piece of wax paper. Stand grater over paper and grate onion half (*or*, instead, chop it *very* finely with knife). Discard or cut up last pieces of onion so you don't grate your fingers. You should have about 3 tablespoons (45 ml) onion. Add grated onion to beaten eggs.

5. After potatoes have drained at least 5 minutes, add them to egg-onion mixture in large bowl. Preheat oven to 350° F (175° C).

6. Remove melted margarine from stove and stir it into egg-potato mixture. Stir in salt, pepper, baking powder, and potato starch.

7. Spoon potato mixture into greased baking dish. Place dish in preheated oven and set timer to bake 50 to 60 minutes. Kugel is done when top looks golden-brown. Remove from oven with potholders. Serve hot. Leftover kugel can be reheated or sliced and fried until crisp.

FRUIT COMPOTE

As fruit compote can be made a day or more in advance, it is traditionally served as a Sabbath dinner dessert. It is a delicious treat with any meal and may be served alongside main-dish meats or roasts as well as a sweet at meal's end. In Israel, compotes are usually made with fresh fruits. This recipe can be made with either fresh *or* preserved fruits, *or* a combination of both—in fact, you can vary the ingredients to suit whatever you have in the house.

EQUIPMENT:

Large saucepan with lid
Measuring cups and spoons
Paring knife and cutting board
Timer
Long-handled fork
Wooden spoon

FOODS YOU WILL NEED:

1 box (11 ounces) dried apricot halves (2 cups; 300 g)

1 cup seedless raisins, regular *or* golden (250 ml; 160 g)
6 dried prunes, pitted style
2 whole pears
3 large eating apples
1 lemon
1 stick cinnamon
4 tablespoons granulated sugar *or* honey (60 ml)
3 cups water (750 ml)

Ingredients:

(To make 10 half-cup servings [125 ml])

1 box (11 ounces) dried apricot halves (2 cups; 300 g)
1 cup seedless regular *or* golden raisins (250 ml; 160 g)
6 dried prunes, pitted, cut into quarters
2 whole pears, cores and stems removed, cut in thick slices
3 large apples, peeled, cored, cut in thick slices
1 lemon, cut in half; slice one half into thin crosswise cartwheels and squeeze juice of other half into a measuring cup. Remove pits.
1 stick cinnamon
4 tablespoons granulated sugar *or* honey (60 ml)
3 cups water (750 ml)
NOTE: Add *or* substitute fresh *or* canned and drained peaches, plums, cherries.

How To:

1. Use any or all of the fruits listed. Prepare fruits as indicated at the left. Place all fruits in saucepan along with cinnamon stick, sugar *or* honey, water, and lemon juice. Cover pan and set it on stove over medium heat. Bring mixture to a boil, then reduce heat to low and simmer fruits about 10 minutes, *or* until fruit is tender when stuck with a long-handled fork. Turn off heat.

2. Let fruit stand in pan until cold. Taste juice and add more sugar *or* honey if necessary. Chill compote until serving time if you like, *or* serve it warm. (Remove lemon slices before serving if you wish.)

Rosh Hashanah

Rosh Hashanah is the New Year, literally, "Head of the Year," celebrated on the first two days of Tishri (September–October). These two days are the most sacred period of the year, the High Holy Days, a time of prayer and self-judgment that ushers in the Ten Days of Penitence, during which God reviews our lives and writes His judgment in the Book of Life.

At home, the New Year is ushered in with many symbolically special foods. Fresh apple slices are dipped in honey, Apple Cake,* Honey Cake,* and honey pastry (*teiglach*) all signify wishes for a "sweet year." Sweet dishes are preferred, sour or bitter flavors avoided. Challah* is baked in a round form on Rosh Hashanah to symbolize the whole, round year. The round challah (see Contents for Challah) is sometimes decorated with dough ladders and birds to help prayers rise up to God. First fruits and vegetables of the fall harvest are always on the Rosh Hashanah menu. *Tsimmes** is a popular dish because it contains sweet potatoes as well as carrots, whose Yiddish name (*meyrin*) means "to increase," as one wishes the New Year to increase in goodness.

A Rosh Hashanah menu might include apple slices dipped in honey, Challah,* gefilte fish, Chicken Soup* with Kreplach,* Meat Tsimmes,* Honey Cake,* and fresh fruits.

ROSA QUEEN'S TSIMMES

This recipe for tsimmes, a pungent and delicious pot roast casserole, comes from my favorite great aunt. Russian in origin, it is made with carrots, sweet potatoes, prunes, and meat. Other versions of the recipe contain only vegetables and dried fruits. The word *tsimmes* (tsim'-mes) comes from the German *zum* "to the" and *essen* "eating." Since tsimmes contains lots of mixed-up ingredients, the word has also come to mean "something mixed up," "a big fuss or mess." "What a big tsimmes that was!" you might say about something very troublesome (but *not* about this easy-to-follow recipe). NOTE: Tsimmes cooks about 1½ to 2 hours, so plan your time accordingly.

EQUIPMENT:

Vegetable peeler
Paring knife and cutting board
Measuring cups and spoons
Dutch oven *or* other deep pot with lid
Long-handled fork
Wooden spoon
Wax paper
Small bowl
Timer

FOODS YOU WILL NEED:

1 medium-sized yellow onion
2 tablespoons vegetable oil (30 ml)
4 medium-sized white potatoes
4 medium-sized sweet potatoes
4 large carrots
15 dried prunes, pitted style
2 pounds beef brisket *or* chuck (1 kg)
1 to 2 cups water (250 to 500 ml)
½ teaspoon cinnamon (2.5 ml)
½ to 1 teaspoon salt (2.5 to 5 ml)
¼ teaspoon pepper (1.2 ml)
1 tablespoon brown sugar (15 ml)
1 tablespoon honey (15 ml)
3 tablespoons lemon juice (45 ml)
1½ tablespoons flour (22 ml)

Ingredients:

(To make 5 to 6 servings)

1 medium-sized yellow onion
2 tablespoons vegetable oil (30 ml)

How To:

1. Peel onion. Chop it into small pieces (see Basic Skills) on cutting board. Place oil in Dutch oven *or* pot and add chopped onions. Set pot on stove over medium-low heat and fry onions until golden. Stir them occasionally with wooden spoon. While onions cook, prepare step 2.

4 medium-sized white potatoes
4 medium-sized sweet potatoes
4 large carrots
15 dried prunes, pitted style

2 pounds beef brisket *or* chuck (1 kg)
1 cup water (250 ml)

2. Peel all potatoes. Cut them into quarters. Peel carrots and cut them into crosswise slices about ¼″ thick (0.5 cm). Set prunes, potatoes, and carrots aside on a piece of wax paper.

3. When onions are golden, remove pot from stove and turn off heat. Spoon onions into small bowl. Return pot to stove and set over medium heat. Add meat, cut up into 2 *or* 3 large pieces to fit it flat in the pot. Brown meat on both sides, turning it with long-handled fork. When browned, sprinkle on the cooked onions and add the water. Cover pot and turn heat to medium-low, set timer for 1 hour.

½ teaspoon ground cinnamon (2.5 ml)
½ teaspoon salt (2.5 ml)
¼ teaspoon pepper (1.2 ml)
1 tablespoon packed brown sugar (15 ml)
1 tablespoon honey (15 ml)
3 tablespoons lemon juice (45 ml)
1½ tablespoons flour (22 ml)

To Make Sauce

5. In small bowl mix cinnamon, salt, pepper, brown sugar, honey, lemon juice, and flour. Stir well, then spoon about 4 tablespoons (60 ml) hot pot juice into sauce bowl. Stir well until lumps are gone. Pour this mixture back into pot on top of meat, potatoes, carrots, and prunes.

4. After meat has cooked one hour, it is time to test it by poking with a long-handled fork. *Ask an adult to help test doneness.* When meat has cooked enough to feel tender, turn off heat under pot. Use fork to push meat to one side of pan and add the potatoes, carrots, and prunes. Be sure potatoes are sitting in pot liquid. If there is very little liquid left, add another cup or so of water. Recover pan, then turn heat on under pot to medium and set timer to cook 1 more hour, *or* until meat *and* vegetables are tender and done through when poked with long-handled fork.

6. When sauce is slightly thickened, turn off heat under pot. Taste sauce. Flavor should be a strong, evenly balanced sweet/sour. Add more brown sugar *or* lemon juice *or* salt if needed. Serve tsimmes hot, combining all ingredients in each serving. If you reheat tsimmes and gravy gets too thick, thin it slightly with a little orange juice.

HONEY CAKE

Honey is always a part of the Rosh Hashanah celebration because it symbolizes the sweetness wished for the New Year. Whenever you smell this honey cake baking, you will know for sure that Rosh Hashanah has arrived.

EQUIPMENT:
2 loaf pans, 9″ × 5″ × 3″ (23 × 12.5 × 7.5 cm)
Saucepan
Measuring cups and spoons
Mixing spoon
Medium and large mixing bowls
Sifter
Electric mixer *or* eggbeater
Rubber scraper
Timer
Cake tester *or* toothpick
Potholders
Platter

FOODS YOU WILL NEED:
1½ tablespoons margarine (22 ml)
1½ cups honey (375 ml)
1 cup strong coffee (250 ml)
3½ cups all-purpose flour (875 ml; 580 g)
Pinch of salt
1 teaspoon baking soda (5 ml)
2 teaspoons baking powder (10 ml)
4 eggs
2 tablespoons vegetable oil (30 ml)
1 cup granulated sugar (250 ml; 210 g)
1 teaspoon cinnamon (5 ml)
½ teaspoon ground nutmeg (2.5 ml)
¼ teaspoon ground cloves (1.2 ml)
⅛ teaspoon ground ginger (0.5 ml)

Ingredients:

(To make 2 loaves, each 9″ × 5″ × 3″; 23 × 12.5 × 7.5 cm)

1½ tablespoons margarine (22 ml)

1½ cup honey (375 ml)

1 cup strong coffee (250 ml)

How To:

1. Grease loaf pans with margarine. Turn oven on to 325° F (165° C).

2. Measure honey into saucepan and set it on stove over medium heat. Cook *just until* honey comes to a boil. Do not allow honey to continue boiling. Then remove pan from heat and set on heat-proof surface to cool.

3. Measure 1 cup (250 ml) strong coffee *or* mix 1½ teaspoons (7.5 ml) instant coffee with 1 cup (250 ml) very hot water. When honey is cooled a little, stir in coffee. Set mixture aside.

3½ cups all-purpose flour (875 ml; 580 g)

Pinch of salt

1 teaspoon baking soda (5 ml)

2 teaspoons baking powder (10 ml)

4 eggs

2 tablespoons vegetable oil (30 ml)

1 cup granulated sugar (250 ml; 210 g)

1 teaspoon cinnamon (5 ml)

½ teaspoon ground nutmeg (2.5 ml)

¼ teaspoon ground cloves (1.2 ml)

⅛ teaspoon ground ginger (0.5 ml)

4. Sift flour, salt, baking soda, and baking powder into medium bowl and set aside.

5. One at a time, break eggs into a measuring cup, pick out any bits of shell, then add eggs to large mixing bowl. Add oil and sugar and beat well with electric mixer *or* eggbeater. Then add cinnamon, nutmeg, cloves, and ginger and beat again.

6. Place bowl of flour mixture and honey-coffee pan alongside large bowl of egg-sugar mixture. Add about 2 tablespoons (30 ml) flour mixture to egg-sugar mixture and beat well. Then pour in about ¼ cup (60 ml) honey-coffee and beat again. Finally, add all remaining flour and honey-coffee mixtures alternately, about ¼ cup (60 ml) at a time. Beat between each addition.

7. Spoon or pour batter into greased loaf pans. They should each be about ⅔ full. Use rubber scraper to empty bowl.

8. Place pans in preheated 325° F (165° C) oven and set timer for 55 to 65 minutes. Cakes are done when tester stuck in center comes out clean. Use potholders to remove pans from oven and set on heat-proof surface. Let cakes stand until cold. Then turn them over onto a platter and remove them from pans.

MARIA PETERDI'S APPLE KUCHEN

This Hungarian specialty uses sour cream in the batter, to make one of the most delicious cakes we know. Top the cake with apple slices for a traditional kuchen, *or* use halved plums to make **Hungarian Plum Cake.**

EQUIPMENT:

Pie plate *or* cake pan, 10″ (25.5 cm) diameter
Teacup
Measuring cups and spoons
Medium and large mixing bowls
Electric mixer *or* mixing spoon
Sifter
Vegetable peeler
Knife and cutting board
Timer
Toothpick *or* cake tester
Potholders
Spatula

FOODS YOU WILL NEED:

1 cup butter *or* margarine (250 ml; 240 g), at room temperature—NOTE: butter gives best flavor
1 egg
1¼ cups granulated sugar (310 ml; 265 g)
⅓ cup sour cream (80 ml) *or* plain yogurt
2 cups all-purpose flour (500 ml; 325 g)
½ teaspoon baking powder (2.5 ml)
⅛ teaspoon salt (0.5 ml)
5 to 6 medium-sized apples (0.5 kg) *or* about 1 pound plums (0.5 kg) (prune-type preferable)

Topping—optional:

3 tablespoons wheat germ (45 ml) *or* all-purpose flour
½ cup chopped walnuts (125 ml; 65 g)
1 teaspoon cinnamon (5 ml)
1 teaspoon ground nutmeg (5 ml)

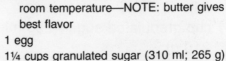

Ingredients:

(To make one 10″ cake [25.5 cm])

1 teaspoon butter *or* margarine (5 ml)

1 egg
¾ cup butter *or* margarine (1½ sticks; 185 ml); at room temperature
1 cup granulated sugar (250 ml; 210 g)
⅓ cup sour cream *or* plain yogurt (80 ml)

How To:

1. Turn oven on to 350° F (175° C). Grease pan with butter *or* margarine.

2. Separate egg (see Basic Skills), putting white in cup for another use and adding yolk to large bowl. Add margarine *or* butter, sugar, and sour cream *or* yogurt. Beat with mixer *or* spoon.

2 cups all-purpose flour (500 ml; 325 g)

½ teaspoon baking powder (2.5 ml)

⅛ teaspoon salt (0.5 ml)

5 to 6 medium-sized apples (0.5 kg) *or* about 1 pound plums (0.5 kg)

3 tablespoons butter *or* margarine (45 ml)

3 tablespoons wheat germ *or* all-purpose flour (45 ml)

¼ cup granulated sugar (60 ml)

½ cup walnuts, shelled and finely chopped (125 ml; 65 g)

1 teaspoon cinnamon (5 ml)

1 teaspoon ground nutmeg (5 ml)

To Make Crumb Topping—Optional

7. Combine margarine *or* butter, wheat germ *or* flour, sugar, nuts, cinnamon, and nutmeg in medium-sized bowl. Blend mixture together with your fingers, squeezing and pinching dry ingredients into the shortening. Mixture should make crumbs smaller than peas. Sprinkle crumbs evenly over fruit in pan. NOTE: Omit topping if you prefer.

8. Place pan in 350° F (175° C) oven and set timer to bake 40 to 45 minutes, or until cake is golden around edges and toothpick *or* tester placed in *side* of cake's top comes out clean. Remove pan with potholders and place on

3. Wash your hands, as you will be touching dough. Sift flour, baking powder, and salt directly into bowl on top of yolk mixture. Beat slowly at first, then beat harder until dough is well blended and holds together in a soft ball. Dough should be softer than cookie dough and slightly less dry; if it feels too sticky, add more flour (up to ½ cup [125 ml]).

4. Flour your hands. Press dough onto greased pan, pushing it all over bottom and up pan sides. Dough should be an even thickness all around—roughly ¼" (0.5 cm).

5. Wash, dry, and peel apples. Cut them into slices about ¼" to ⅛" thick (0.5 to 0.25 cm). Discard cores. If using plums, wash them, then cut them in half and remove pits. Don't peel plums.

6. Arrange apple slices in slightly overlapping rows covering all the dough in the pan. If using plums, push each half, *skin side down,* into the dough in neatly arranged all-over pattern.

APPLES

APPLES

← PLUMS

heat-proof surface to cool. Serve directly from baking pan, cutting cake in squares lifted out with spatula.

Yom Kippur

Yom Kippur is the "Day of Atonement," the last of the Ten Days of Repentance begun on Rosh Hashanah. This is the most solemn day of the year, a fast day for adults and children over thirteen. One spends the day in prayer, making peace with enemies and settling one's conscience with God.

Before sundown on the eve of Yom Kippur, the family eats a big dinner. This is a filling meal, meant to see one through the next day without food. After this meal, nothing is eaten until sundown the next day.

When the final sounding of the *shofar* (ram's horn) announces the end of the holiday, families leave the synagogue and return home to break their fast. Usually, they begin with a light snack, such as Challah* and Chopped Liver,* or tea and Rugalach,* or Apple Kuchen.* Later, a full meal is served, and may include Chicken Soup* with Kreplach,* roast poultry, Fruit Compote,* salad, *Zimsterne* Cookies,* and fresh fruit.

KREPLACH

M

Definitely related to Oriental dumplings and *wonton,* kreplach (kre'-plah) probably originated in China and were brought to Europe from Asia by Jewish tea traders. Kreplach are pockets of dough filled with various mixtures of meat, cheese, or kasha. Our recipe contains chicken or beef filling and is traditionally served floating in Chicken Soup* to break the Yom Kippur fast.

EQUIPMENT:
Frying pan
Chopping board and knife
Measuring cups and spoons
Wooden spoon, mixing spoon, slotted spoon
Large mixing bowl
Pastry board—optional
Wax paper
Rolling pin
Ruler
Table knife, spoon, fork
Large pot *or* Dutch oven with lid
Timer
Wire rack set on jelly roll pan *or* in platter
    with lip
Deep fat fryer—optional
Paper towels

FOODS YOU WILL NEED:
2 tablespoons margarine (30 ml)
½ small yellow onion
1 cup raw *or* cooked chicken *or* lean hamburger (250 ml)
1¾ teaspoons salt (8.7 ml)
½ teaspoon pepper (2.5 ml)
1 cup all-purpose flour (250 ml; 165 g)
1 egg
1 tablespoon water (15 ml)

Ingredients:

(To make 24 kreplach)

2 tablespoons margarine (30 ml)
½ small yellow onion
1 cup raw *or* cooked chicken *or*
    lean hamburger (250 ml)

How To:

To Make Filling

1. In frying pan, melt margarine on stove over low heat. While this is melting, chop onion (see Basic Skills) very finely. Add onion to pan with melted margarine. Cook over medium heat until onions are golden. Stir with wooden spoon. Whether using cooked *or* raw chicken, chop it up very finely. If meat is already cooked, add it to cooked onions.

(37)

½ teaspoon salt (2.5 ml)
½ teaspoon pepper (2.5 ml)

1 cup all-purpose flour (250 ml;
    165 g)
1 egg
¼ teaspoon salt (1.2 ml)
1 tablespoon water (15 ml)

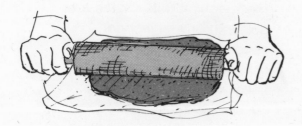

If chicken *or* hamburger is raw, add it to cooked onions and cook together in frying pan until meat is done through. (Hamburger will be brown and chicken tender.) Remove from heat and set pan aside to cool mixture.

To Make Dough

2. Measure flour into bowl, make hole in flour and add egg, salt, and water. With fork *or* spoon, mix well until dough forms a ball. Remove dough from bowl, set it on lightly floured board *or* work surface, and knead dough by folding it over toward you then pushing it away while leaning on it with the heels of your hands. Give dough a quarter turn and repeat the folding and pushing. Add a little more flour if dough continues to feel sticky. Knead about 25 times, until dough feels elastic and smooth. Break ball in half; wrap one half in wax paper and set it aside.

3. Place second half of dough on lightly floured board *or* piece of wax paper. Rub a little flour on a rolling pin. Roll dough (see Basic Skills) as thin as you can from center to outer edges. This will be hard to do at first as dough seems to be rubbery, but keep at it, occasionally turning dough over and stretching it gently between your hands. Do not rip

Water
1 teaspoon salt (5 ml)

dough. Finally, the dough thins out and holds its shape; it should be about $1/16''$ (0.12 cm) thick and form a square *or* circle roughly 9″ to 10″ (23 to 25 cm). NOTE: If you have a pasta machine, this dough can be put through the smooth rollers until a thin, lasagnalike strip is produced.

4. Use a table knife to cut dough into 2½″ (6 cm) squares. Place 1 teaspoon (5 ml) of filling in the center of each square. Set a cup of water nearby. Dip a finger in the water and dab it on all inner edges of dough. Then fold dough over into a triangle, stretching dough slightly as you pull it over the filling. Pinch dampened edges together. Seal edges by pressing along them with tines of fork. Set all completed kreplach on a lightly floured board.

5. When ready to cook, fill a large pot about ⅔ full of water, add 1 teaspoon (5 ml) salt. Cover pot and bring water to boil on stove over high heat.

6. *Ask an adult to help with this step.* When water is boiling, set kreplach on slotted spoon and lower them gently—a few at a time—into boiling water. (Boil them in two or three batches, not all at once.) Set timer for 20 minutes. While they are cooking, set wire rack on tray *or* jelly roll pan. When time is up, lift kreplach out of water with slotted spoon and set them on rack to drain.

7. To serve kreplach in the traditional way, drop previously boiled kreplach into hot chicken soup and simmer them about 15 minutes, or until thoroughly heated. Serve 2 or 3 in each bowl of soup.

   If you want to fry kreplach, heat about 1″ (2.5 cm) oil in frying pan *or* prepare a deep fat fryer. *Ask an adult to help.* When oil is hot enough to brown a bread crust in about a minute, use slotted spoon and set *previously boiled and drained* kreplach down *gently* into hot oil. Fry them 2 to 3 minutes on each side, or until golden-brown. Drain on paper towels *or* a brown bag and serve hot as hors d'oeuvres *or* as a main course.

AUNT BELLE'S RUGALACH

This flaky cream cheese pastry can have a variety of fillings and be formed into many different shapes. Traditionally, rugalach (ru'-ga-la) are cookie-sized crescents rolled over a mixture of cinnamon-nuts *or* poppy seeds.

EQUIPMENT:
Cookie sheet
Large, medium, and small mixing bowls
Mixing spoon
Measuring cups and spoons
Wax paper
Ruler
Table knife, fork, spoon
Eggbeater
Pastry brush
Timer
Potholders
Wire rack
Sifter

Nut Filling:
½ cup walnuts, ground *or* finely chopped (125 ml; 65 g)
¼ cup granulated *or* brown sugar (60 ml; 55 g)
½ teaspoon cinnamon (2.5 ml)
¼ teaspoon ground nutmeg (1.2 ml)
1 egg white, beaten

FOODS YOU WILL NEED:

Pastry:
1 cup plus 2 tablespoons, butter *or* margarine (280 ml; 270 g), at room temperature
2 eggs, plus 1 egg white
8 ounces cream cheese (227 g), at room temperature
Pinch of salt
2 teaspoons sour cream *or* plain yogurt (10 ml)
2 cups all-purpose flour (500 ml; 325 g)
1 teaspoon granulated sugar (5 ml)

Poppy Seed Filling:
½ cup poppy seeds (125 ml; 80 g)
6 tablespoons walnuts, ground *or* very finely chopped (90 ml)
6 tablespoons granulated *or* brown sugar (90 ml)

Jelly *or* Jam Filling:
Any variety, about ½ cup (125 ml)
Confectioners' sugar

Ingredients:

(To make about 48 crescents)

2 tablespoons butter *or* margarine (30 ml)
2 eggs (if you are not making nut filling, you only need 1 egg)

How To:

1. Grease cookie sheet with butter *or* margarine. Separate eggs (see Basic Skills). Put one yolk in large mixing bowl and save second yolk for another use; put whites in small bowl to be set aside.

1 cup butter *or* margarine (250 ml; 240 g), at room temperature

8 ounces cream cheese (227 g), at room temperature

Pinch of salt

2 teaspoons sour cream *or* plain yogurt (10 ml)

2 cups all-purpose flour (500 ml; 325 g)

1 teaspoon granulated sugar (5 ml)

2. In large bowl, use mixing spoon to beat egg yolk with butter *or* margarine and cream cheese. When well blended, stir in salt, sour cream *or* yogurt, flour, and sugar. Mix well until dough will form a ball. Add a little more flour if needed. Wrap ball in wax paper and refrigerate it while preparing the filling.

3. Prepare nut and/or poppy seed filling by mixing each group of ingredients together in separate medium-sized bowls. If you plan to use jelly *or* jam as well, set it nearby.

4. Turn oven on to 375° F (190° C). Remove dough from refrigerator. Work with about ⅓ of dough at a time. Roll out a lump of dough on lightly floured pastry board *or* between sheets of wax paper (see Basic Skills). Roll until dough is about ⅛″ (0.25 cm) thick (slightly thicker than pie crust). Cut with knife into 4″ × 4″ (10 × 10 cm) squares for crescents, or 2″ (5 cm) squares for envelopes.

CRESCENTS

5. Add extra egg white to those in bowl and beat slightly with fork. To make crescents, brush larger squares with egg white, then sprinkle on about 1 teaspoon (5 ml) nut *or* poppy seed mixture. Roll up diagonally, from one corner to the corner opposite, as shown. Bend roll down into

curved crescent and set on cookie sheet. Use pastry brush to brush tops of finished shapes with more egg white and sprinkle on a little sugar.

To make envelopes, brush egg white on smaller, 2″ (5 cm) squares of dough. Drop about ½ teaspoon (2.5 ml) filling *or* jelly *or* jam in center. Pinch 2 opposite points together as shown, holding points with dab of egg white. Set on cookie sheet and brush tops with more egg white. Place cookie sheet in oven at 375° F (190° C) and set timer to bake 15 to 20 minutes, or until pastry is golden in color.

6. Use potholders to remove cookie sheet from oven. Set on heat-proof surface. Lift rugalach with spatula and set them on wire rack placed over a piece of wax paper. When rugalach are cooled, sift confectioners' sugar lightly over jelly-filled envelopes. Leave crescents plain.

ENVELOPES

MUFFIN'S BUTTER COOKIES D or p

This is our all-time favorite cookie recipe. The dough may be mixed and shaped entirely by hand, so it is fun for even the youngest member of the family. Cornstarch in the dough gives it an especially crisp and tender texture, and the flavor is very buttery. For Yom Kippur in Israel, the cookies are traditionally shaped in the form of stars, sprinkled with cinnamon, and called *Zimsterne* (stars, in Yiddish). Serve them when the stars come out, to break the fast after sundown. NOTE: This recipe contains no eggs and thus is suitable for restricted or low-cholesterol diets.

EQUIPMENT:
Cookie sheet
Measuring cups and spoons
Large mixing bowl
Mixing spoon
Sifter
Table fork
Pastry brush—optional
Spatula
Timer
Wire rack
Airtight container

FOODS YOU WILL NEED:
¾ cup plus 1 teaspoon *cold* butter *or* margarine (190 ml; 305 g)—Note: For pareve cookies, use only kosher margarine.
1 teaspoon vanilla extract (5 ml)
1 teaspoon almond extract (5 ml)
½ cup cornstarch (125 ml; 65 g)
½ cup confectioners' sugar (125 ml; 65 g)
1 cup all-purpose flour (250 ml; 165 g)
Optional: 1 beaten egg for glaze, cinnamon, jam, halved nuts, chocolate bits *or* kisses, seedless raisins

Ingredients:

(To make about 25 to 30 cookies)

1 teaspoon butter *or* margarine (5 ml)

¾ cup *cold* butter (for best flavor) *or* margarine (185 ml)
1 teaspoon vanilla extract (5 ml)
1 teaspoon almond extract (5 ml)
½ cup cornstarch, sifted (125 ml; 65 g)
½ cup confectioners' sugar, sifted (125 ml; 65 g)
1 cup all-purpose flour, sifted (250 ml; 165 g)

How To:

1. Grease cookie sheet with butter *or* margarine. Turn oven on to 325° F (165° C). Wash your hands as you will be touching the dough.

2. Break up the butter *or* margarine into small bits and place in mixing bowl. Add vanilla and almond extract. Measure and sift in cornstarch, confectioners' sugar, and flour directly over butter mixture. Use a mixing

spoon *or*, if you prefer, your hands to squeeze and pinch the flour and butter together. The heat of your hands will soften the butter after a short while, and the dough will start to stick together. Keep working until dough is well blended and forms a ball easily. If dough feels too soft, chill it awhile in refrigerator. NOTE: Margarine is softer than butter and with it you may need to add from ½ to 1 cup (125 to 250 ml) more flour to form a dough ball that is not too sticky to handle.

3. For Yom Kippur, roll dough between your hands into 6″ (15 cm) long ropes about ½″ (1 cm) thick. To form stars bend ropes into triangles that overlap as shown. Pat a drop of water or beaten egg under points where triangle legs cross.

   Or, instead, add a tablespoon *or* two more flour to stiffen dough and roll it out with a rolling pin (see Basic Skills), then cut stars with a cookie cutter. Brush cut stars with a beaten egg and sprinkle them lightly with cinnamon.

4. To shape regular cookies, break off lumps of dough roughly 1″ (2.5 cm) in diameter and roll them into balls between your palms. Set balls an inch or so apart on greased cookie sheet. You can now flatten dough balls with fork tines dipped into flour *or*, instead, make a "well" in the center of each dough ball with the tip of your finger. Fill the well with a piece of chocolate, a nut *or* raisin, *or* a drop *or* two of jam. For another variation, you can add ½ cup (125 ml) finely chopped nuts to dough in step 2.

5. Set cookie sheet in 325° F (165° C) oven and set timer to bake regular cookies for about 20 minutes, or until lightly golden around edges. Rolled and cut cookies bake 12 to 15 minutes. Remove from oven with potholders and cool on wire rack.

PRESS FORK TINES

BALL

WELL

FILL THE WELL

Succot

Succot, the autumn "Feast of the Ingathering," or harvest, is celebrated on the fifteenth and sixteenth days of Tishri (September–October). The holiday honors the first fruits of the harvest and recalls the little booths, or *succahs,* the Jews lived in while wandering in search of a home after the Exodus from Egypt centuries ago. Thus, Succot is also called "Festival of the Booths."

This time of thanksgiving begins five days after Yom Kippur and lasts eight days. Some families make their own little outdoor *succah*, or booth, decorated with branches, grapevines or leaves, and fresh fruits. During the holiday in Israel and other countries, many families eat their meals inside the *succah*.

Harvest foods such as Stuffed Grape or Cabbage Leaves* or Stuffed Peppers* are traditionally served. Other Succot specialities are Fruit Compote,* fresh fruit salad, Tsimmes* made with carrots and sweet potatoes (meat may be left out and apples and nuts added), Date-Nut Balls,* and fruit and nut cakes (see Index).

The seventh day of Succot is *Hoshanah Rabbah,* a day celebrated with a special religious service in which a procession marches seven times around the synagogue. Members of the congregation carry willow branches, which they beat; the falling leaves symbolize the arrival of spring rains and the hope of renewed life. After this service, families return home for a festive meal that traditionally includes *Kreplach** (dough pockets stuffed with savory meat) as part of the main course.

The eighth day of Succot is *Shemini Azeret,* "Assembly on the Eighth Day," when special synogogue services include prayers for rain and remembrance of the dead.

The ninth day after Succot is *Simhat Torah,* the day of "Rejoicing in the Torah." On this day, the reading of the Torah is completed for the year and immediately begun again, symbolizing that study of the Torah has no end. There is a gay celebration in the temple on this day. Adults and children share in the Torah readings and in a procession. They follow the rabbi and cantor, both carrying Torahs, as they parade around the synagogue. The young people carry Israeli and Simhat Torah flags decorated with apples topped with candles, signifying "the fruit and light of the Torah."

MOTHER'S STUFFED CABBAGE OR PEPPERS

Stuffed cabbage *or* peppers is a Succot treat for Jewish families around the world. Some claim that the dish originated in Russia, but both Poland and Romania proudly claim this particular sweet-and-sour-flavored recipe as their own. As variations, you can also cook plain meatballs in the same sauce, or fill grape leaves with the meat mixture.

EQUIPMENT:
2 Dutch ovens *or* other large pots (6-quart *or* 6 liter-size) with lid
Measuring cups and spoons
Long-handled wooden spoon
Large mixing bowl
Wax paper
Paring knife and cutting board
Colander
Timer
Potholders
Clean dishtowel
Toothpicks

1 (10¾-ounce) can Campbell's Tomato Soup (with water added as directed on can) *or* equivalent size can of Kosher tomato sauce
16-ounce can whole tomatoes (not Italian style)
½ cup seedless raisins (125 ml; 80 g)
¼ cup lemon juice (60 ml; 1½ lemons)
3 to 5 tablespoons brown sugar (45 to 75 ml)
1 whole green cabbage *or* 8 to 10 whole bell peppers
1 pound hamburger (0.5 kg)
½ cup uncooked white rice (125 ml; 100 g)
½ teaspoon salt (2.5 ml)
½ teaspoon pepper (2.5 ml)
½ cup water (125 ml)

FOODS YOU WILL NEED:
1 yellow onion
3 tablespoons cooking oil (45 ml)

Ingredients:

(To make 10 pieces of stuffed cabbage or *8 to 10 stuffed peppers)*

1 yellow onion
3 tablespoons oil (45 ml)
1 (10¾-ounce; 305 g) can Campbell's Tomato Soup (with 1 can water added) *or* equivalent size of Kosher tomato sauce
1 (16-ounce; 454 g) can whole tomatoes
½ cup seedless raisins (125 ml; 80 g)
¼ cup lemon juice (60 ml; 1½ lemons)
3 tablespoons brown sugar (45 ml)

How To:

To Make Sauce

1. Make sauce first so it can simmer while meat is prepared. First, peel and chop onion (see Basic Skills). Add oil to Dutch oven *or* large pot, and set pot on stove over medium-low heat. Add chopped onion and sauté (cook slowly) until golden in color. Stir with wooden spoon. When onion is golden, turn off stove heat. Add soup, can of whole tomatoes and their juice, raisins, lemon juice, and brown sugar. Stir well. Taste

NOTE: Peppers do not have to be cooked before stuffing; cabbage must be cooked first. If you are making stuffed *cabbage,* **skip** step 7. If making stuffed *peppers,* **follow** steps 1, 3, 7, and 8.

1 whole green cabbage *or* 8 to 10 whole bell peppers
1 pound hamburger (0.5 kg)
½ cup uncooked white rice (125 ml; 100 g)
½ teaspoon salt (2.5 ml)
½ teaspoon pepper (2.5 ml)
½ cup water (125 ml), approximately

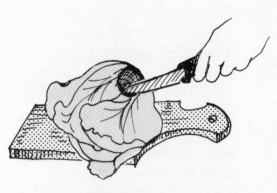

sauce. It should have an evenly balanced, strong sweet-sour flavor. Add more lemon juice *or* more sugar if needed. Return pot to low heat on stove, cover with lid, and simmer until meat is ready.

2. Half-fill second large pot with water. Set pot on stove over high heat, cover with lid, and bring to boil while following step 3, preparing meat.

To Make Meat Stuffing

3. First, wash your hands. Combine hamburger, rice, salt, pepper, and water (see Note) in large bowl. NOTE: Add water a little at a time, adding just enough to make mixture light, but not too loose to form balls. Stir mixture with fork *or* spoon.

4. If using cabbage, *ask an adult to help with this step.* First, cut the core (stem) out of the bottom of the cabbage head as shown, using paring knife. Throw core away. *Ask adult* to set whole head of cabbage into boiling water. Set timer for 10 minutes.

5. When cabbage is cooked, turn off heat on stove. Set colander in sink. *Ask adult* to carry pot to sink and pour cabbage out into colander. Turn your head to avoid steam. Run cold water over

cabbage to cool it. Carefully separate and peel off 10 *whole* leaves. Place leaves on dishtowel to cool. Save rest of cabbage for a soup or other use.

6. Set each cabbage leaf one at a time on cutting board. Cut a wedge-shaped piece about 1½″ to 2″ (5 cm) deep from core end (a). Set leaf cut-edge down and place about a tablespoon of meat just above cut as shown (b). Adjust amount of meat to fit size of leaf. Roll up bottom of leaf (c), covering meat. Fold sides over (d), then roll down the top of the leaf to close the envelope. Fasten cabbage to itself with a toothpick (e). Set stuffed envelopes on large spoon and lower them carefully into the sauce.

7. To stuff peppers: Wash each pepper, then use paring knife to cut off the top around stem. Pull out white membrane and all seeds. Fill each pepper with meat mixture. Set stuffed peppers on large spoon and carefully lower them into sauce, standing peppers open-end-up in pan.

8. Return pan to stove-top. Cover with lid and set pan over medium-low heat. Simmer slowly for about 60 minutes (set timer). When done, ask adult to remove heavy pot from stove and set it on heat-proof surface. Serve hot, with sauce.

ANNE STERNBERGER'S MANDLEBROT

These raisin-nut biscuits are a traditional Succot treat, although they make a perfect snack any day of the year. Because mandlebrot (mahn'-del-brot) are crisp and dry, they keep well either frozen or stored in an airtight container.

EQUIPMENT:
Cookie sheet
Large, medium, and small mixing bowls
Sifter
Measuring cups and spoons
Nut chopper *or* knife and cutting board
Electric mixer *or* mixing spoon
Timer
Spatula
Knife (serrated *or* bread-type)
Wire rack
Airtight container

FOODS YOU WILL NEED:
½ cup plus 2 tablespoons margarine (155 ml), at room temperature
3¾ cup all-purpose flour (935 ml; 620 g)
3 teaspoons baking powder (45 ml)
¼ teaspoon salt (1.2 ml)
1 cup blanched almonds (250 ml; 135 g)
1 cup golden *or* regular seedless raisins (250 ml; 160 g) *or* ½ cup raisins plus ½ cup candied fruits
1 cup granulated sugar (250 ml; 210 g)
4 eggs
1 teaspoon vanilla extract (5 ml)
1½ teaspoons almond extract (7.5 ml)

Ingredients:

(To make about 36 biscuits)

2 tablespoons margarine (30 ml)

3¾ cup all-purpose flour (935 ml; 620 g)

3 teaspoons baking powder (45 ml)

¼ teaspoon salt (1.2 ml)

1 cup blanched almonds (250 ml; 135 g)

1 cup golden *or* regular seedless raisins (250 ml; 160 g) *or* ½ cup raisins plus ½ cup candied fruits

How To:

1. Grease cookie sheet with margarine and set it aside. Turn oven on to 350° F (175° C).

2. In medium-sized bowl, sift together flour, baking powder, and salt. Set bowl aside.

3. Chop nuts into small pieces (about ¼"; 0.5 cm). Measure nuts and raisins (and/or fruit) into small bowl. Add about 2 tablespoons (30 ml) of flour mixture from step 2 and stir it around with nuts and fruits. Set bowl aside.

½ cup margarine (125 ml; 120 g), at room temperature

1 cup granulated sugar (250 ml; 210 g)

4 eggs

1 teaspoon vanilla extract (5 ml)

1½ teaspoons almond extract (7.5 ml)

4. In large bowl, use electric mixer *or* spoon to beat together margarine and sugar. When well blended, add eggs by first breaking them one at a time into the measuring cup to pick out any bits of shell. Add eggs, then vanilla and almond extract and beat well.

5. Wash your hands. Stir flour mixture into margarine-sugar-egg mixture. When well blended, stir in raisin-nut mixture and blend well. Dough should feel quite dry, like cookie dough. If it feels sticky to your hands, sprinkle on a little more flour and stir or knead. When dough feels easy to handle, form it into a ball.

6. Flour your hands. Divide dough ball into 3 equal parts. Form each part into a long flat roll and set it down as shown on the cookie sheet. Slightly flatten the top of each roll. The rolls should be about 14″ long, 2″ to 2½″ wide, and roughly ½″ thick (36 × 6 × 1 cm).

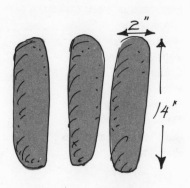

7. Place cookie sheet in 350° F (175° C) oven and set timer to bake 40 to 45 minutes or until dough looks lightly golden on top. Remove pan from oven with potholders and set on heat-proof surface. Let cool about 5 minutes. Use spatula to lift each roll onto cutting board. With sharp knife, cut still-warm rolls into diagonal slices about ¾″ to 1″ thick (2 to 2.5 cm) as shown.

8. Turn oven heat down to 300° F (150° C). Place slices flat on cookie sheet and return them to oven. Set timer for 10 minutes, and toast slices. Then remove them from oven, place on wire rack, and leave until cold and crisp. Store in airtight container.

(49)

LUCY PURDY'S PECAN-APPLE PUDDING   *p or D*

This delicious apple-nut pudding is easy to make and will quickly become a family favorite. NOTE: For a different flavor, you can substitute walnuts for pecans.

EQUIPMENT:
2- *or* 3-quart baking *or* souffle dish (2 liters) *or* 10″ (25.5 cm) pie plate
Large mixing bowl
Measuring cups and spoons
Eggbeater *or* electric mixer
Large spoon
Nut chopper *or* knife and board
Vegetable peeler
Grater
Wax paper
Rubber scraper
Timer
Cake tester *or* toothpick
Potholders

FOODS YOU WILL NEED:
1 tablespoon margarine (15 ml)
2 eggs
1 cup granulated sugar (250 ml; 210 g)
4 tablespoons all-purpose flour (60 ml; 40 g)
2 teaspoons baking powder (10 ml)
½ teaspoon salt (2.5 ml)
1 cup pecans, shelled (250 ml; 115 g), *or* walnuts
3 medium-sized apples (1 cup grated; 250 ml)
1 teaspoon vanilla extract (5 ml)

Topping—optional:
1 cup heavy cream (250 ml)
3 tablespoons granulated sugar (45 ml)

Ingredients:

(To make 4 to 6 servings)

1 tablespoon margarine (15 ml)

2 eggs
1 cup granulated sugar (250 ml; 210 g)

4 tablespoons all-purpose flour (60 ml; 40 g)
2 teaspoons baking powder (10 ml)
½ teaspoon salt (2.5 ml)

How To:

---

1. Turn oven on to 350° F (175° C). Grease baking dish with margarine.

2. One at a time, break eggs into measuring cup, pick out any shell bits, then add to large bowl. Add sugar and beat well until a light yellow color.

3. Add flour, baking powder, and salt to egg mixture. Beat well.

1 cup pecans, shelled (250 ml; 115 g), *or* walnuts

4. Chop, cut, *or* break up pecans (*or* walnuts) into small pieces. Stir nuts into egg-flour mixture. Stir in vanilla and mix well.

3 medium-sized apples
1 teaspoon vanilla extract (5 ml)

5. Wash and peel apples. Grate apples over a piece of wax paper, using medium-small holes of grater. Discard apple cores. You should have about 1 cup (250 ml) or more grated apple. Stir apple into egg-flour-nut mixture.

6. Use rubber scraper to push batter from bowl into greased baking dish. Place dish in 350° F (175° C) oven and set timer to bake for 35 to 45 minutes, or until cake tester stuck into pudding center comes out clean. *(Ask an adult to help test in hot oven.)* When done, remove from oven with potholders. Set dish on heat-proof surface.

7. Serve pudding warm *or* cold. If you wish to make this a dairy dish, beat heavy cream until stiff, then stir in granulated sugar. Serve as topping for pudding.

FLAKY PIE CRUST

This easy-to-make *pareve* pastry may be served with either dairy or meat dishes. You can use your favorite pie fillings, *or* try our suggestion: Apricot-Walnut Pie,* which follows.

EQUIPMENT:
Sifter
Large bowl
Measuring cups and spoons
Pastry blender *or* 2 table knives
Wax paper *or* pastry board
Table fork
Rolling pin

FOODS YOU WILL NEED:
2 cups all-purpose flour (500 ml; 325 g)
1 teaspoon salt (5 ml)
⅔ cup margarine *or* Crisco (160 ml)
⅓ cup cold water (80 ml)

Ingredients:

(To make top and bottom crust for 9″ [23 cm] pie)

2 cups all-purpose flour (500 ml; 325 g)

1 teaspoon salt (5 ml)

⅔ cup margarine *or* Crisco (160 ml)

⅓ cup cold water (80 ml)

How To:

1. Sift flour and salt into large bowl. Add margarine *or* Crisco and mix with pastry blender *or* by making crosscutting motion with 2 table knives. Blend until dough lumps are smaller than pea-sized.

2. Sprinkle most—but not all—water over flour mixture. Use fork to blend in water until dough is thoroughly damp and will form a ball. Add more water if necessary. Dough should not be sticky; neither should it feel too dry and crumbly. When dough feels right, form ball, roll it in wax paper, and refrigerate until ready to roll out and fill. (Refrigeration is *not* essential.)

3. To complete pie crust, divide dough into 2 equal balls. Roll out one on a floured pastry board *or* between 2 sheets of wax paper (see Basic Skills). Roll from center toward edges to make circle. Test size by setting pie plate facedown over dough; crust should stick out about 2″ (5 cm) beyond rim. Set bottom crust evenly into pan and gently press out any air bubbles. Add filling. Roll top crust as above.

4. Cut a hole about ½" (1 cm) diameter in center of top crust to let out steam. Set top crust evenly over filling. Moisten edges of lower crust with finger dipped in cold water. Press crust edges together. To seal them, *flute* by pinching edge of dough between thumb and forefinger of one hand while poking forefinger of other hand into space between them as shown (a), *or* press tines of table fork dipped in flour into edge all around (b). Bake as directed by your filling recipe.

APRICOT-WALNUT PIE   p *or* D

Although this is a very rich pie, the filling is tart rather than sweet, and covered with a crunchy layer of caramelized custard and chopped nuts. For the pastry, use half the recipe for *pareve* Flaky Pie Crust (see Index). For a *pareve* pie, omit milk *or* cream in custard; for a dairy meal, add it. The pie is even more spectacular when served topped with a tablespoon of vanilla yogurt, ice cream, *or* whipped cream.

EQUIPMENT:
Medium-sized saucepan with lid
Measuring cups and spoons
Timer
Strainer
2 medium-sized mixing bowls
9" (23 cm) pie plate
Rolling pin
Wax paper *or* pastry board
Mixing spoon
Nut chopper *or* knife and cutting board
Eggbeater *or* wire whisk
Potholders

FOODS YOU WILL NEED:
1 box (11-ounces) dried apricot halves (3 cups; 311 g)
2 cups water (500 ml)
Pastry (½ recipe for Flaky Pie Crust, see Index)
½ cup walnuts, shelled (125 ml; 65 g)
2 eggs
1 cup granulated sugar (250 ml; 210 g)
1 teaspoon vanilla extract (5 ml)
⅛ teaspoon cinnamon (0.5 ml)
3 tablespoons cream *or* milk (45 ml)— optional

Ingredients:

(To make one 9" [23 cm] pie)

1 box (11-ounces) dried apricot
   halves (3 cups; 311 g)
2 cups water (500 ml)

2 eggs
½ cup granulated sugar (125 ml;
   105 g)
1 teaspoon vanilla extract (5 ml)
⅛ teaspoon cinnamon (0.5 ml)
3 tablespoons cream *or* milk (45
   ml)—optional

½ cup granulated sugar (125 ml;
   105 g) or more, to taste

How To:

1. To prepare apricots, measure them into saucepan and cover with water. Put lid on pan and set it on stove over medium-high heat until water boils. Reduce heat slightly and boil gently for about 15 minutes (set timer). Apricots are done when they feel soft when pricked by a fork. While they are cooking, prepare pastry and custard in steps below. When apricots are done, remove from heat and pour them into a strainer set over a bowl. Drain juice and let apricots cool. (Save juice to drink later.)

2. Prepare ½ recipe for Flaky Pie Crust (see Index). Roll out dough (see Basic Skills) and fit it into pie pan. To make a neat edge, pinch dough into an even-sized lip all around rim as shown. (There is no top crust.)

½ cup walnuts, shelled (125 ml; 65 g)

3. Turn oven on to 375° F (190° C). Chop nuts finely and set them aside on piece of wax paper.

4. In bowl, beat together eggs, sugar, vanilla, cinnamon, and cream *or* milk if used. Set mixture aside.

5. Return drained apricots to original saucepan and stir in sugar. Add more if too tart for your taste. Then spoon out apricots in an even layer on prepared pie crust. Sprinkle on chopped nuts, then pour the egg mixture over top.

6. Set pie plate in 375° F (190° C) oven and set timer for 20 minutes. After that, reduce heat to 325° F (165° C) and set timer for 40 to 50 minutes, or bake until crust is golden. If crust does not look browned when time is up, increase oven heat to 350° F (175° C) and bake 10 more minutes. Remove from oven with potholders. Cool before serving.

Hanukah

Hanukah is celebrated for eight days, beginning on the twenty-fifth day of Kislev (November–December). The holiday celebrates a victory for religious freedom. It honors Judas Maccabeus, who in 165 B.C. led his small band in a rebellion that drove out the army of the Syrian king, Antiochus. The king's soldiers had overrun the Temple of Jerusalem and dedicated it to Greek gods. When the Maccabees entered the temple, they wanted to rededicate it by lighting the *menorah* (candelabrum). They could find only a tiny container of oil; miraculously, this oil burned for eight days. For this reason, Hanukah is known as the "Festival of Lights."

It is celebrated in Jewish homes by the lighting of candles on the menorah every evening for eight days. This is a gay and festive holiday, with songs, games, and an exchange of gifts on each of the eight days. Potato Pancakes* *(Latkes)* are traditionally served, as are confections made of fruits, nuts, and sesame seeds (Sesame Seed Candy*). To make Hanukah Dreydl (dray'-del) Cookies, follow recipe for Muffin's Butter Cookies.* Copying our sketches cut a cardboard pattern of a dreydl about 3″ (8 cm) tall. Roll out dough (add more flour if necessary) and cut around pattern. Frost cookies after baking.

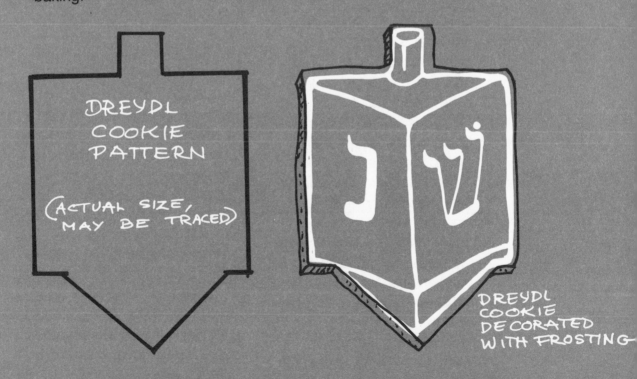

DREYDL COOKIE PATTERN

(ACTUAL SIZE, MAY BE TRACED)

DREYDL COOKIE DECORATED WITH FROSTING

GREAT-GRANDMA SOPHIA'S
POTATO PANCAKES (*LATKES*)

When you think of a Hanukah party, you naturally think of potato pancakes, or *latkes* (lat'-kes). This traditional recipe is easily prepared in your blender, and party serving is made easy when cooking is done right at the table on an electric frying pan. Serve *latkes* hot, accompanied by apple sauce.

EQUIPMENT:
Vegetable peeler
Paring knife and cutting board
Electric blender *or* grater
Wax paper
Rubber scraper
Measuring cups and spoons
Strainer
Medium and large mixing bowls
Large spoon
Electric frying pan *or* regular frying pan
Pancake turner

FOODS YOU WILL NEED:
5 or 6 medium-size white potatoes
1 medium-sized yellow onion
2 eggs
1 teaspoon salt (5 ml)
⅛ teaspoon ground pepper (0.5 ml)
2 tablespoons matzoh meal *or* unsweetened cracker crumbs, crushed (30 ml)
Margarine *or* butter for frying
Applesauce—optional side dish

Ingredients:

(*To make 12 to 16* latkes)

5 or 6 medium-sized white potatoes

1. Use vegetable peeler to peel potatoes. Discard skins. If using blender, cut peeled potatoes into ½" (1 cm) cubes. Add about ⅓ cup (80 ml) cubes to blender at a time. Cover container and turn motor on for several 3- or 4-second spurts. Set strainer over medium bowl. Pour blended potatoes into strainer using rubber scraper to push them out. Repeat, blending all potatoes *just for a few seconds,* so pieces are slivered as if they were grated, *not* ground into a smooth liquid. Allow all potatoes to drain in strainer at least 5 minutes.

How To:

2. If using a grater, hold peeled potatoes against medium-sized holes of grater set on top of a piece of wax paper. Keep your fingers well back from holes. When you reach the last bit of potato, do not grate it; instead, chop it with a knife, so you don't get fingers too near the grater. Place all grated potato in strainer set over bowl; let potatoes drain at least 5 minutes. NOTE: Do not worry if potatoes turn brownish in color after a while. This happens when they are exposed to the air, but does not change the flavor. If you will not be using the potatoes right away, cover them with plastic wrap.

1 medium-sized yellow onion

2 eggs
1 teaspoon salt (5 ml)
⅛ teaspoon pepper (0.5 ml)

2 tablespoons matzoh meal *or* unsweetened cracker crumbs, crushed (30 ml)

Margarine *or* butter

5. Add matzoh meal *or* cracker crumbs to egg-onion mixture in bowl. Stir. Add drained potatoes from strainer and stir well again.

6. Turn electric frying pan on to 350° F (175° C), *or* set regular frying pan on stove over medium-high heat. Add a tablespoon (15 ml) of margarine *or* butter. When margarine sizzles, add the potato batter, one heaping tablespoon at a time for each pancake. You may need additional fat. Cook on the first side about 4 minutes, or until golden-brown, then turn over pancake and fry till crisp brown on other

3. Peel onion and discard skin. If using blender, cut onion into quarters and blend them for a few seconds, then add ingredients in step 4.

    If *not* using blender, grate or very finely chop onion (see Basic Skills) and put pieces into large bowl.

4. If using blender, add eggs, salt, and pepper to onion in blender container. Blend a few seconds, until well ground. Turn off motor, use rubber scraper to remove mixture from blender to large bowl.

    If *not* using blender, add eggs, salt, and pepper to onion bits in bowl and beat them together well with large spoon.

side. Serve pancakes immediately or keep them warm on an oven-proof platter in a warm oven until ready to serve. (Spread them in a single layer if in oven or they will steam and get soggy.) Serve pancakes with a side dish of cold applesauce.

ZAIDA JOSEPH'S MAMALIGA p

A cornmeal pudding, *mamaliga* (ma-ma-li'-ga) is the Romanian national dish—as basic to that cuisine as pasta is to that of the Italians. The following recipe was a favorite of my Romanian great-grandfather, Joseph. My father recalls the reverence and awe with which he and his three small brothers watched their bearded *zaida* (grandfather) perform the ritual of slicing the corn pudding with a tautly held length of white thread.

EQUIPMENT:
Measuring cups and spoons
Large saucepan with lid
Long-handled wooden spoon
Timer
Wooden cutting board *or* platter
Table knife
White thread
Drinking glass

FOODS YOU WILL NEED:
4 cups water (1 liter)
1 teaspoon salt (5 ml)
2 cups yellow cornmeal (500 ml)
3 tablespoons butter *or* margarine (45 ml)

Ingredients:

(To make 4 to 6 servings)

4 cups water (1 liter)
1 teaspoon salt (5 ml)

2 cups yellow cornmeal (500 ml)

3 tablespoons butter *or* margarine (45 ml)

How To:

1. Measure water and salt into saucepan. Cover and set on high heat on stove until water boils.

2. *Ask an adult to help with this step.* Turn heat down low under water, so it boils very gently. *Ask an adult* to pour cornmeal into boiling water while stirring with wooden spoon. Stir about 3 minutes, until mixture thickens.

3. After mamaliga thickens, stir in butter *or* margarine. Turn heat down to low, cover pan, and set timer to simmer (cook slowly) 20 to 30 minutes. Pudding is done when it no longer sticks to the sides of the pan when it is stirred.

4. Wash your hands. Rub a little margarine *or* butter over the wooden board *or* platter. Spoon cooked mamaliga out of the pan onto the greased surface. Let it cool about one minute, then mold it with a knife *or* back of spoon dipped in a glass of cold water. Mold it into an oval mound, as shown, roughly 5″ or 6″ long × 1½″ to 2″ thick (15 × 5 cm).

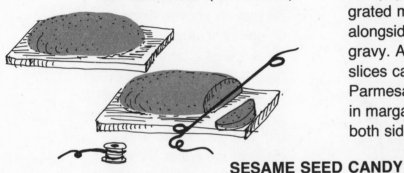

5. To slice your mamaliga the Romanian way, cut a piece of thread about 20″ (51 cm) long. Stretch the thread tightly between your hands and pull it down through the mounded pudding, cutting off slices about ½″ (1 cm) thick. If you prefer, you can slice mamaliga with a sharp knife.

Serve hot slices with salt and pepper, butter and/*or* grated mild cheese, *or* alongside meat, topped with gravy. As a variation, the slices can be dipped in Parmesan cheese, then fried in margarine until browned on both sides.

p
Passover

SESAME SEED CANDY

This recipe has its roots in biblical times, when honey and sesame seeds were served for very special occasions. Sesame seeds today are as traditional for Hanukah as poppy seeds are for Purim. On Passover, turn this recipe into **Sephardic Nut Brittle** (*Ahashoo*) by substituting matzoh farfel for sesame seeds. NOTE: Make this candy only in dry weather. On a rainy day, moisture in the air will keep the candy from hardening properly.

EQUIPMENT:
Large saucepan
Measuring cups and spoons
Candy thermometer *or* glass of ice water
Timer
Long-handled wooden spoon
Nut chopper *or* knife and cutting board
Marble slab *or* wooden board *or* large platter
Knife
Plastic wrap *or* wax paper
Airtight container

FOODS YOU WILL NEED:
1 cup honey (250 ml)
1 cup granulated sugar (250 ml; 210 g)
½ cup water (125 ml)
½ teaspoon cinnamon (2.5 ml)
½ teaspoon ground ginger (2.5 ml)
Pinch of salt
1 cup walnuts, shelled (250 ml; 125 g), *or* almonds, blanched
2 cups sesame seeds, hulled (500 ml; 320 g), *or* for Passover, 2 cups matzoh farfel (250 ml; 135 g)

Ingredients:

*(To make about 50 pieces, ½"
[1 cm] square)*

1 cup honey (250 ml)
1 cup granulated sugar (250 ml;
   210 g)
½ cup water (125 ml)
½ teaspoon cinnamon (2.5 ml)
½ teaspoon ground ginger (2.5
   ml)
Pinch of salt

1 cup walnuts, shelled (250 ml;
   125 g), *or* almonds blanched
2 cups sesame seeds, hulled
   (500 ml; 320 g), *or* for Passover, use 2 cups matzoh farfel
   (250 ml; 135 g)

3. Sprinkle a few drops of water
   over marble slab *or* board *or*
   platter. Then *carefully* pour
   hot candy mixture onto dampened surface. Use back of
   spoon to spread and flatten
   candy to about ⅛" (0.25 cm)
   thickness. Let candy cool
   about 5 minutes. While still
   warm (it gets brittle when
   cold) slice into bite-sized

How To:

1. Measure honey, sugar, water,
   cinnamon, ginger, and salt
   into large saucepan. Place
   pan on stove and set over
   medium heat for about 15 to
   20 minutes. Stir occasionally
   with wooden spoon. Do not let
   honey boil too long or its
   flavor will change.

   If using thermometer, set it
   on pan as shown, tilting it so
   tip does not touch pan bottom.
   Cook mixture until it reaches
   hard ball stage, 240° F (120°
   C) on thermometer, or until a
   drop of syrup turns into a hard
   ball when spooned into a
   glass of ice water. When
   done, *ask an adult to help you*
   lift pan from stove and set it
   on a heat-proof surface.

2. Chop nuts using chopper *or*
   knife on cutting board. With
   wooden spoon, stir chopped
   nuts and sesame seeds (*or*
   matzoh farfel) into cooked
   syrup.

pieces about ½" (1 cm)
square *or* slightly larger.
When cold and brittle, wrap
individual pieces in plastic
wrap. Unwrapped candy will
stick together. Store candy in
airtight container; refrigerate
to harden if it gets soft.

Tu Bishvat

Tu Bishvat, "Israeli Arbor Day," is celebrated on the fifteenth day of Shevat (January–February). This holiday is also known as "New Year of the Trees," or "Holiday of Planting Trees," for in the Middle Eastern climate, this day comes at the beginning of spring. Trees are beginning to bloom and it is picnicking and planting time.

The holiday has its origin in ancient spring agricultural celebrations, and one custom that has come down through the centuries is the tasting of at least fifteen different types of fruits. This number is chosen because the holiday occurs on the fifteenth day of the month.

Today on Tu Bishvat, it is traditional to serve a large variety of fruits—dried, fresh, and in baked goods.

DATE-NUT BALLS

These nutritious fruit candies are perfect to take along on a Tu Bishvat picnic. They are quick and easy to make, using only a hot plate *or* stove-top; no baking oven is required, so this is a good recipe for a school group or club. Candies will keep if stored in a cool place.

EQUIPMENT:
Paring knife and cutting board
Measuring cups and spoons
Saucepan
Long-handled wooden spoon
Nut chopper—optional
Small mixing bowl
Sifter
Airtight container

FOODS YOU WILL NEED:
1 cup pitted dates (250 ml; 200 g)
1 cup brown sugar, packed (250 ml; 250 g)
8 tablespoons butter *or* margarine (125 ml; 120 g)
1 cup walnuts, shelled (250 ml; 125 g)
½ cup dry shredded coconut (125 ml; 80 g)
1½ cups Rice Krispies *or* other cereal (375 ml; 150 g)
½ cup toasted wheat germ (125 ml; 60 g)
¾ cup confectioners' sugar (185 ml; 95 g)

Ingredients:

*(To make about 40 balls 1"
[2.5 cm] in diameter)*

1 cup pitted dates (250 ml; 200 g)

1 cup brown sugar, packed (250 ml; 250 g)

8 tablespoons butter *or* margarine (125 ml; 120 g)

1 cup walnuts, shelled (250 ml; 125 g)

½ cup dry shredded coconut (125 ml; 80 g)

1½ cups Rice Krispies *or* other cereal (375 ml; 150 g)

½ cup toasted wheat germ (125 ml; 60 g)

½ cup confectioners' sugar (125 ml; 65 g), sifted into bowl

How To:

1. Check dates to be sure all pits are removed. Chop dates. Place chopped dates in saucepan.

2. Add brown sugar and butter *or* margarine to saucepan. Set pan on stove over medium-low heat and cook mixture 4 to 5 minutes, *just* until butter melts and sugar dissolves. Stir with wooden spoon to prevent sticking.

3. Chop nuts finely and set them aside. When butter-sugar-date mixture is cooked, stir in nuts, coconut, Rice Krispies, and wheat germ.

4. Wash your hands. When candy mixture in pan is cool enough to handle, pick up small lumps and roll them in your palms, making about 40 balls about 1" (2.5 cm) in diameter. Roll balls in bowl of sifted sugar, then set them down into container. When all balls are in container, sift on remaining sugar.

Purim

Purim, the "Festival of Lots," is celebrated on the fourteenth day of Adar (February–March). It commemorates an event that occurred in ancient Persia when the Jews lived under the domination of King Ahasuerus.

The king was convinced by his wicked minister, Haman, to have all the Jews of the kingdom killed on a day selected by casting "lots" (*pur*). The king's beautiful Jewish wife, Esther, learned of Haman's plot from her uncle Mordecai, the leader of the Jewish community. At the last moment, Queen Esther was successful in persuading the king to issue a new order that allowed the Jews to fight back. They fought, won, and were saved. Haman was hanged on the same gallows he had prepared for Mordecai.

At Purim parties, young people dress in costumes and masquerade, pretending to be Haman, the king, and especially the popular and lovely Queen Esther. Often edible gifts are exchanged, the most common being Purim delicacies such as Hamantashen,* Poppy Seed Cookies,* and homemade Purim confections such as Carrot-Ginger Candy.*

MRS. FIERSTEIN'S HAMANTASHEN   p *or* D

Hamantashen (hah'-men-ta-shen) are traditional Purim pastries filled with a prune (or poppy seed) mixture and shaped into triangular pockets to recall the hat of Haman, the villain of the Purim story.

EQUIPMENT:

Cookie sheet
Mixing bowls: 2 large, 1 medium, 1 small
Measuring cups and spoons
Small frying pan *or* pot
Wire whisk *or* eggbeater
Mixing spoon, wooden spoon, teaspoon
Grater
Sifter
Wax paper
Paring knife, table knife
Nut chopper *or* cutting board
Timer
Food mill—optional
Rolling pin
Cup *or* jar lid 3½" to 4" (8 to 10 cm) in diameter
Spatula
Wire rack

FOODS YOU WILL NEED:

Pastry:
9 tablespoons margarine *or* butter (135 ml)
2 eggs
½ cup granulated sugar (125 ml; 105 g)
2 tablespoons water (30 ml)
1 teaspoon vanilla extract (5 ml)
1 lemon
½ teaspoon baking soda (2.5 ml)
½ teaspoon baking powder (2.5 ml)
Pinch of salt
3 cups all-purpose flour (750 ml; 500 g)
½ cup honey for glaze (125 ml)

Filling:
12-ounce can (1¼ cups; 310 ml) "lekvar" prune butter *or* pastry filling (*or* same quantity of cooked, pitted prunes put through food mill)
1 lemon
½ cup walnuts, coarsely chopped (125 ml; 65 g)
½ cup Corn Flakes, crushed (125 ml)

Ingredients:

(To make about 24 hamantashen)

1 tablespoon margarine *or* butter (15 ml)

8 tablespoons butter *or* margarine (120 ml)

2 eggs
½ cup granulated sugar (125 ml; 105 g)
2 tablespoons water (30 ml)
1 teaspoon vanilla extract (5 ml)

How To:

To Make Pastry:

1. Turn oven on to 375° F (190° C). Grease cookie sheet with margarine *or* butter and set it aside.

2. Place margarine *or* butter in small frying pan *or* pot and set it on stove over low heat to melt. When melted, remove from heat.

3. One at a time, break eggs into a measuring cup, pick out any shell bits, then place eggs in large bowl. Beat eggs with whisk *or* beater, then beat in sugar, melted butter *or* margarine, water, and vanilla.

1 lemon

½ teaspoon baking soda (2.5 ml)
½ teaspoon baking powder
   (2.5 ml)
Pinch of salt
3 cups all-purpose flour (750 ml;
   500 g)

Filling

12-ounce can (1¼ cups; 310 ml)
   "lekvar" prune butter *or* pastry
   filling (*or* same quantity of
   cooked, pitted prunes put
   through food mill)
1 lemon (grate rind, cut into quarters, remove pits, squeeze
   juice into small bowl, finely
   chop pulp)
½ cup walnuts, coarsely
   chopped (125 ml; 65 g)
½ cup Corn Flakes, crushed (125
   ml)

7. Remove dough from re-
   frigerator. Roll out a portion of
   dough on lightly floured pastry
   board or between sheets of
   wax paper (see Basic Skills).
   Roll dough quite thin (less
   than ⅛″ [0.25 cm]).

8. To cut circles of dough, dip
   rim of small cup *or* jar lid into
   flour, then turn it upside down
   and press rim firmly into
   dough (a), while twisting it. Lift
   cup *or* jar lid, leaving cut-out
   circle (b). Repeat, making circles as close together as possible. Pull up dough strips between circles and return them
   to larger ball of dough. Repeat
   with all dough.

4. Set grater over wax paper.
   Grate rind of lemon. Then cut
   lemon in half and squeeze
   juice into cup. Remove pits.
   Add lemon rind and juice to
   egg-butter mixture in bowl.

5. Sift baking soda, powder, salt,
   and flour directly into bowl of
   egg-butter-lemon mixture. Stir
   dough together until it forms a
   ball, feels stiff, and is no
   longer sticky. Add a little more
   flour if needed. Wrap dough in
   wax paper and chill in refrigerator while making filling.

To Make Filling:

6. Place canned prune butter *or*
   milled prunes into large mixing bowl. Add grated lemon
   rind, juice, and chopped pulp
   (pits removed). Add chopped
   nuts and Corn Flakes. Mix
   well.

9. Place about 1 heaping teaspoon of filling (5 ml) in the
   center of each dough circle.
   Flip two sides of circle over
   onto filling (a, b, c). Flip up
   bottom, making triangle (d).
   Pinch dough edges together.
   Seal filling inside. Place completed hamantashen on
   greased cookie sheet. Drip a
   little honey over top of each
   pastry before baking. Place
   sheet in 375° F (190° C) oven.
   Set timer for 12 minutes, or
   bake until pastry is golden on
   top. Set on wire rack to cool.

BEA JOSLIN'S CARROT-GINGER CANDY

These brittle squares of carrot-nut candy, spiced with ginger, are a favorite at Purim as well as on Passover and Hanukah. They are also called *Meyrin ingberlach* (carrot gingers). This candy is best made in dry weather; on rainy days the mixture will not harden properly because of the moisture in the air.

EQUIPMENT:

Vegetable peeler
Wax paper
Grater
Paring knife, chopping board
Lemon squeezer—optional
Teacup
Nut chopper—optional
Measuring cups and spoons
3-quart saucepan
Wooden spoon
Candy thermometer—optional, *or* drinking glass of ice water
Wooden board *or* marble slab *or* large flat platter
Plastic wrap
Airtight container

FOODS YOU WILL NEED:

1½ pounds raw carrots (about 7 *or* 8 carrots; 725 g)
2 lemons
1 cup walnuts, shelled (250 ml; 125 g), *or* almonds, blanched
2 cups granulated sugar (500 ml; 420 g)
½ cup water (125 ml)
1 teaspoon ground ginger (5 ml)

Ingredients:

(To make about 100 pieces of candy ¾" [2 cm] square)

1½ pounds raw carrots (about 7 *or* 8 carrots; 725 g)

2 lemons

How To:

1. Wash carrots, then peel them with vegetable peeler. Set grater over wax paper. Grate carrots using medium-size holes of grater. Leave grated carrots on paper, set aside, until ready to use.

2. Wash lemons. Over a second piece of wax paper, grate rind of one lemon. Leave rind on paper and set it aside. Cut grated lemon in half, remove pits, and squeeze juice into teacup. Also cut second lemon in half and squeeze its juice into same cup. Remove any pits from juice.

1 cup walnuts, shelled (250 ml; 125 g), *or* almonds, blanched

2 cups granulated sugar (500 ml; 420 g)
½ cup water (125 ml)
1 teaspoon ground ginger (5 ml)

3. Chop nuts very finely, working with about ¼ cup (60 ml) at a time. Set nuts aside in measuring cup.

4. In saucepan, combine sugar, water, ginger, and lemon rind and juice that were set aside. Stir with wooden spoon, then stir in grated carrots from step 1.

5. Set pan on stove over medium heat and bring to gentle boil. Cook about 20 to 30 minutes, or until all liquid is boiled out. If you have a candy thermometer, set it in the pan to guide you. Tilt it slightly on the pan so the tip doesn't touch pan bottom. As mixture cooks, it will turn brown in color. Stir it occasionally with wooden spoon. *Ask an adult to help, or supervise, as splashes can burn.* If you do not have a thermometer set a glass of ice water alongside stove. When thermometer reaches 240° F (120° C), hard ball stage, *or* when a drop of syrup gets hard when set into ice water, turn off heat. Remove pan from stove and set on heat-proof surface. At once, stir in chopped nuts and mix well.

6. Dampen board *or* slab *or* platter lightly with a few drops of cold water. Use wooden spoon to pull candy mixture out of pan and spread it on dampened surface. Flatten candy with dampened back of spoon. Form a rough square of approximately 12" (30.5 cm), about ⅛" (0.25) thick. While candy is still warm, cut it into ¾" (2 cm) squares. Let stand until hard and brittle—about an hour or longer (on a cool, dry day). Wrap each piece in plastic wrap and store airtight.

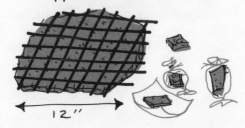

12"

RACHEL'S POPPY SEED COOKIES   p or D

Simple to make and simply delicious, these cookies are a traditional part of any Purim celebration. Make plain butter cookies by leaving out the poppy seeds (but not on Purim!).

EQUIPMENT:
Small frying pan
Cup
Large mixing bowl
Measuring cups and spoons
Electric mixer *or* mixing spoon
Rubber scraper
Cookie sheet
Table fork
Timer
Spatula

Wire rack
Potholders

FOODS YOU WILL NEED:
1 cup (2 sticks) margarine *or* butter (for best flavor) (250 ml; 240 g)
2 eggs
1 cup granulated sugar (250 ml; 210 g)
1 teaspoon vanilla extract (5 ml)
Pinch of salt
2 tablespoons poppy seeds (30 ml; 20 g)
3 cups all-purpose flour (750 ml; 500 g)

Ingredients:

(To make about 48 cookies)

1 cup (2 sticks) margarine *or* butter (250 ml; 240 g)

2 eggs

1 cup granulated sugar (250 ml; 210 g)

1 teaspoon vanilla extract (5 ml)
Pinch of salt

2 tablespoons poppy seeds (30 ml; 20 g)

3 cups all-purpose flour (750 ml; 500 g)

6. Wash hands. With your fingers, break off walnut-sized lumps of dough and roll them into balls. Set balls on *ungreased* cookie sheet. Dip table fork into flour, then press tines onto each ball to flatten.

7. Set sheet of cookies into 350° F (175° C) oven and set timer to bake 10 to 12 minutes, or until lightly golden in color.

How To:

1. Turn oven on to 350° F (175° C).

2. Measure margarine *or* butter into small frying pan and set it on stove over low heat until melted. Remove from heat and allow to cool slightly.

3. While margarine *or* butter is melting, separate 2 eggs (see Basic Skills) and put whites in cup for another use. Put yolks in large mixing bowl. Beat in sugar, vanilla, and salt.

4. Add poppy seeds to batter in bowl. With rubber scraper, add melted and cooled margarine *or* butter to batter. Beat well.

5. Add flour, one cup (250 ml) at a time. Beat slowly at first, then harder, until well mixed.

Passover

Passover, or *Pesach*, the "Festival of Unleavened Bread," is celebrated for seven or eight days, from the fifteenth to the twenty-first or twenty-second of Nisan (March–April). Almost four thousand years ago, the Hebrew tribes in Egypt were enslaved by the pharaoh. Passover celebrates the time when Moses led the Exodus of the Jews out of Egypt, out of bondage. Thus, Passover is also called the "Festival of Freedom."

During the Exodus, the Jewish people fled in great haste. They took their bread dough without letting it rise, and baked it quickly in the sun, while still flat. Matzoh, unleavened bread, reminds us of this flight and struggle. No leavened food *(chometz)* is allowed in Jewish homes on Passover.

Only special foods are permitted during this holiday. Matzohs are allowed, not only because they recall the Exodus, but because they are prepared from wheat specially ground and guarded so it does not touch water or leavening until just ready to be baked. Then it is quickly mixed with water, shaped, and baked without allowing time for any fermentation. Ground-up matzoh is made into matzoh meal as well as matzoh cake meal. Potato starch is also allowed for cooking, as the potato is a vegetable, not a grain. No regular grain products are eaten. Neither baking powder, baking soda, yeast, nor cornstarch may be used, nor any legumes (beans, lentils, peas, and so forth), garlic, or any malt liquors. Especially prepared packaged foods marked *Kosher l'Pesach* are allowed. In Kosher homes, special dishes and utensils are saved exclusively for Passover use.

On the first two evenings of Passover, there is a special feast called a *Seder* (which means "order"). The Seder follows the order of the *Haggadah,* a book that tells the history of the Exodus from Egypt in stories, prayers, and songs. Children participate, ask questions, play games, and learn the meaning of the symbolic foods.

In the center of the Seder table, a special plate displays a roasted lamb bone and roasted eggs, symbolizing the ancient paschal sacrifices; *maror,* the bitter herbs (horseradish) recall the suffering of the Jewish slaves; *Charoses** (an apple-nut mixture) looks like the mortar used to build the pharaoh's pyramids; salt water symbolizes the tears of the slaves, and *karpas* (celery or parsley greens) represents hope and new life brought by the spring.

A special goblet of wine placed on the table is known as the "cup of Elijah," and a door is left ajar during the Seder so the good prophet Elijah may come inside to drink and symbolically herald the coming of the Messiah. Adults drink four ceremonial glasses of wine during the Seder; young people substitute Passover grape juice.

Three specially wrapped pieces of matzoh are in the center of the table. One piece, called the *afikomen* (from the Greek word for "dessert"), is secretly hidden by the head of the family, and after the Seder, the children hunt to find it. Those who are lucky sell their piece back to the head of the family in exchange for small gifts.

A traditional Seder menu may include Chopped liver,* hard-boiled eggs (symbolizing new life in the spring) in salt water, carrot and celery sticks, gefilte fish, Chicken Soup* with Matzoh Balls,* roast poultry, Potato Kugel,* vegetable Tsimmes* (meat omitted), salad, matzohs, fresh fruits, and sweets such as Nut Torte,* or Sponge Cake.*

NANCY'S MATZOH BREI

p *or* D
Passover

Serve Matzoh Brei (mah'-tzah bry) for breakfast, brunch, or lunch. This easy-to-make matzoh-and-egg treat is a traditional Passover favorite.

EQUIPMENT:
2 medium-sized mixing bowls
Measuring cups and spoons
Whisk *or* eggbeater
Strainer
Fork
Frying pan

FOODS YOU WILL NEED:
2 whole sheets matzoh
2 cups cold water (500 ml)
2 eggs
½ teaspoon salt (2.5 ml)
Margarine *or* butter for frying

Ingredients:

(To make 3 or 4 servings)

2 whole sheets matzoh
2 cups cold water (500 ml)

2 eggs
½ teaspoon salt (2.5 ml)

Margarine *or* butter

How To:

1. Break matzoh into small pieces and place them in one bowl. Pour water over matzoh. Set bowl aside.

2. One at a time, break eggs into measuring cup, pick out any shell bits, then pour eggs in second bowl. Add salt. Beat eggs well with whisk *or* eggbeater.

3. Place strainer over sink *or* set it in an empty pan *or* bowl and pour in soaked matzoh and water. Let it sit a minute or two to drain, then push down gently on the matzoh to force out excess water. Lift strainer and pour drained matzoh into beaten eggs. (Throw away drained water.) Stir eggs and matzoh together with fork.

4. Place about 1 tablespoon (15 ml) margarine *or* butter in frying pan. Set pan on stove over medium heat. When fat sizzles, add egg-matzoh mixture and cook while stirring with a fork as you would scrambled eggs. *You may want to ask an adult to help with the cooking.* Mixture is done when it looks dry and is a golden-brown color. Turn off stove. Spoon mixture onto serving dishes and serve hot, topped with a dash of salt *or* sugar.

MOTHER'S MATZOH BALLS

M *or* p
Passover

The real test of a Jewish cook is his or her ability to make light, fluffy matzoh balls. The worst thing that can happen is to hear the cry "cannonballs!" as the first bite is tasted. Yours won't be cannonballs if you follow my mother's recipe. There is no magic to it, just practice for a while to get the "feel" of the batter. Try it and surprise your family and yourself. Serve Matzoh Balls in Chicken Soup* on Passover, the Sabbath, or any other day of the year. NOTE: Matzoh balls may be frozen in a container of soup; they stay light and flavorful when thawed and reheated.

EQUIPMENT:
Mixing bowl
Eggbeater *or* whisk
Measuring cups and spoons
Small frying pan
Dutch oven *or* large soup pot with lid
Slotted spoon
Timer
Small dish

FOODS YOU WILL NEED:
4 eggs
⅓ cup chicken fat [see Basic Skills]
    or shortening (60 ml) for *pareve*
½ cup club soda *or* water (125 ml)
3 teaspoons salt (15 ml)
Pinch of pepper
1 cup matzoh meal (250 ml; 150 g)

Optional:
½ teaspoon fresh dill *or* parsley, finely
    chopped (2.5 ml) *or* ¼ teaspoon same
    herb dried (1.2 ml)

Ingredients:

(To make 10 to 12 matzoh balls)

4 eggs

⅓ cup chicken fat (bottled *or* home-rendered [see Basic Skills]) *or* shortening (60 ml)

½ cup club soda *or* water (125 ml)
1 teaspoon salt (5 ml)
Pinch of pepper
Optional: ½ teaspoon fresh dill *or* parsley, finely chopped (2.5 ml) *or* ¼ teaspoon same herb, dried (1.2 ml)
1 cup matzoh meal (250 ml; 150 g)

6. Lower heat under pot liquid so it is boiling gently. *Ask an adult to help you* set balls on slotted spoon and gently lower them into hot liquid. Place cover on pot. Set timer for 20 minutes. When time is up, remove one ball with slotted spoon and set it on small dish. Taste for doneness. If still hard in center, cook remaining balls a little longer.

7. If balls are cooked in soup, leave them there and serve them immediately. If balls are cooked in water, *ask an adult to help you* lift cooked balls from water with slotted spoon and transfer them to pot of hot soup for immediate serving.

How To:

1. Break eggs into measuring cup, pick out any shell bits, then put eggs in mixing bowl. Beat eggs well and set aside.

2. Set chicken fat *or* shortening in small frying pan and place on stove over low heat to melt. When melted, turn off stove and set pan on heat-proof surface.

3. To eggs in bowl, add soda *or* water, melted fat, salt, and pepper, and—if you like—dill *or* parsley. Beat well. Then add matzoh meal and beat well again. Place bowl in refrigerator for about 60 minutes.

4. Matzoh balls may be cooked either in salted water *or* hot chicken soup. To cook in water, fill pot ⅔ full of water a few minutes before removing batter from refrigerator. Add about 2 teaspoons (10 ml) salt to water, cover pot, and set it on stove over high heat. Bring water to a boil. Or, if you prefer, use a pot of chicken soup.

5. Wash your hands. Remove chilled batter from refrigerator. Wet your hands with *cold* water, then dip your wet fingers into the batter and scoop out a lump about as big as 2 heaping tablespoons (30 ml). Pat batter between your wet palms to form a ball. Balls should hold their shape well, but not be totally stiff and dry.*

*If they do not hold their shape, return batter to refrigerator awhile.

CHAROSES
(Ashkenazic and Sephardic)

Charoses (hah-roh'-ses) is present at the Passover Seder because it symbolizes the mortar used by the Jewish slaves building pyramids for the Egyptian pharaoh centuries ago. The first recipe, a tasty mixture of chopped apples and nuts, is Ashkenazic in origin, coming from the Jewish people of eastern and northern Europe.

The second recipe is pronounced *haroset* and is made of dates instead of apples, but it has the same symbolic meaning as the first. Sephardic *haroset* originated with the Jews from Spain, Portugal, Morocco, Tunisia, Turkey, Greece, and Egypt. Whether you call it *charoses* or *haroset,* you serve it spread on a cracker-sized piece of matzoh for Passover or a year-round snack.

ASHKENAZIC CHAROSES

EQUIPMENT:
Vegetable peeler
Paring knife and cutting board
Medium-sized mixing bowl
Nut chopper—optional
Measuring cups and spoons
Serving bowl

FOODS YOU WILL NEED:
1 medium-sized eating apple
½ cup walnuts, shelled (125 ml; 65 g)
¼ teaspoon cinnamon (1.2 ml)
Pinch of ground ginger
3 tablespoons sweet Concord wine (45 ml)
    or Passover grape juice

Ingredients:

(To make 1 cup mixture [250 ml]—5 or 6 servings; double recipe to serve 12)

1 medium-sized eating apple

½ cup walnuts, shelled (125 ml; 65 g)

¼ teaspoon ground cinnamon (1.2 ml)

Pinch of ground ginger

3 tablespoons sweet Concord wine (45 ml) *or* Passover grape juice

How To:

1. Wash and peel apple. Remove core and discard it. Chop apple into pieces about ¼" (0.5 cm) big. Place apples in bowl.

2. Finely chop walnuts with knife *or* nut chopper. Add nuts to apples in bowl. Add cinnamon, ginger, and wine *or* grape juice. Stir and place in serving bowl. Chill.

EQUIPMENT

Measuring cups and spoons
Saucepan with lid
Timer
Wooden spoon
Grater
Wax paper
Citrus Juicer—optional
Paring knife and board *or* nut chopper
Strainer
2 medium-sized mixing bowls

FOODS YOU WILL NEED:

½ pound pitted dates (8-ounce package;
   227 g)
¾ cup water (185 ml)
1 orange
½ cup walnuts, shelled (125 ml; 65 g)
⅛ teaspoon cinnamon (0.5 ml)
2 tablespoons sweet Concord wine (45 ml)
   or Passover grape juice

Ingredients:

(To make about 1 cup mixture [250 ml]—5 or 6 servings; double recipe for 12)

½ pound pitted dates (8-ounce package; 227 g)
¾ cup water (185 ml)

1 orange
½ cup walnuts, shelled (125 ml; 65 g)
⅛ teaspoon cinnamon (0.5 ml)
2 tablespoons sweet Concord wine (45 ml) *or* Passover grape juice

3. Set strainer in second mixing bowl and place in sink. After dates are cooked, remove saucepan from stove and pour the date mixture directly into the strainer. Allow all water to drain (2 or 3 minutes), then lift strainer and dump drained dates back into empty saucepan. Discard date water. Beat cooked dates with wooden spoon until they become a soft jamlike mixture. Stir dates into orange-nut mixture in bowl. Chill.

How To:

1. Be sure all pits are removed from dates. Place dates in saucepan, add water, and cover with lid. Place pan on stove over medium heat. Bring water to a boil, then reduce heat slightly and cook about 10 minutes (set timer). Stir once or twice with wooden spoon. While dates are cooking, prepare step 2.

2. Wash and dry orange. Set grater on a piece of wax paper and grate the rind of about half the orange. Set paper with rind aside. Cut orange in half and squeeze juice of one half into mixing bowl. Remove pits. Save other half orange for another use (use rind and the juice of whole orange if doubling recipe).

   Chop nuts and place them in bowl with orange juice. Add orange rind, cinnamon, and wine *or* grape juice.

ANNE MAIDMAN'S NUT TORTE

p
Passover

This easy-to-make nut cake can be frosted with a dusting of powdered sugar and served cut in individual squares like brownies. Nut torte freezes well when wrapped airtight in foil *or* plastic.

EQUIPMENT:
8" *or* 9" (20 *or* 23 cm) square baking pan
Wax paper
Pencil
Scissors
Nut mill *or* blender
Large and medium-sized mixing bowls
Measuring cups and spoons
Large mixing spoon
Sifter
Rubber scraper
Electric mixer *or* eggbeater
Timer
Cake tester *or* toothpick

Knife
Cake rack *or* platter

FOODS YOU WILL NEED:
1 tablespoon margarine (15 ml)
¾ cup shelled and/*or* ground walnuts
    (185 ml; 95 g)
4 eggs
½ cup granulated sugar (125 ml; 105 g)
¼ cup honey (60 ml)
¼ cup orange juice (60 ml)
¼ teaspoon cinnamon (1.2 ml)
½ teaspoon salt (2.5 ml)
¾ cup matzoh meal (185 ml; 113 g)
1 tablespoon confectioners' sugar (15 ml)

Ingredients:

(To make about 16 two-inch [5 cm] square servings)

1 tablespoon margarine (15 ml)

¾ cup walnuts, shelled (185 ml; 95 g)

How To:

1. Grease pan with some of the margarine. Then turn pan wrong-side up over a piece of wax paper and draw around pan edges. Cut out paper with scissors. Press paper into greased pan bottom. Use remaining margarine to grease paper. Turn oven on to 350° F (175° C).

2. Grind walnut meats with a nut mill (see sketch) *or* in blender. Pieces should be quite fine, like a coarse meal. Set aside ground nuts on piece of wax paper.

(75)

4 eggs
½ teaspoon salt (2.5 ml)

½ cup granulated sugar (125 ml;
    105 g)
¼ cup honey (60 ml)
¼ cup orange juice (60 ml)
¼ teaspoon cinnamon (1.2 ml)
¾ cup matzoh meal (185 ml;
    113 g)

1 tablespoon confectioners'
    sugar (15 ml)

6. Pour *or* spoon batter into prepared pan. Place pan in 350°
   F (175° C) oven and set timer
   to bake 35 to 45 minutes, or
   until a cake tester poked into
   cake center comes out clean.
   Top of cake will feel springy to
   the touch when done. Use
   potholders to remove cake
   from oven. Let cake cool on
   heat-proof surface. When
   cold, loosen cake from pan by
   sliding a knife between cake
   and pan sides. Turn cake out
   upside down on cake rack *or*
   platter and peel off the wax
   paper. Before serving, sift
   about 1 tablespoon (15 ml)
   confectioners' sugar over top.
   Serve cake cut in 2″ (5 cm)
   squares.

3. Separate eggs (see Basic
   Skills), placing 4 yolks in large
   bowl and 4 whites in medium
   bowl. Beat whites with electric
   mixer *or* eggbeater. Add salt
   when whites are foamy, then
   beat until peaks of foam stand
   upright without drooping and
   are very stiff. Set bowl aside.

4. Beat yolks together. Then
   beat in sugar, honey, orange
   juice, and cinnamon. Sift in
   matzoh meal, then stir in
   ground nuts.

5. Fold egg-nut mixture into
   stiffly beaten whites. To do
   this, spoon nut mixture into
   whites a little at a time and
   turn spoon over and upside
   down through mixture to
   blend. Stir gently as you want
   to keep as much air as possible in the whites to make the
   cake light. Fold until well
   blended. Clean out bowl with
   rubber scraper.

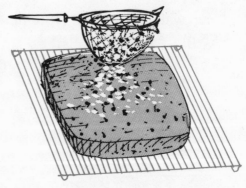

PASSOVER SPONGE CAKE

This traditional Passover Sponge Cake, flavored with lemon and orange, is the perfect light dessert to follow the elaborate Seder meal.

EQUIPMENT:
Bottle (over which to hang inverted tube pan)
9″ (23 cm) tube pan
Two large and one small mixing bowls
Measuring cups and spoons
Sifter
Grater
Citrus juicer
Wax paper
Electric mixer *or* eggbeater
Mixing spoon
Rubber scraper
Cake tester *or* toothpick
Timer

Potholders
Knife
Serving plate

FOODS YOU WILL NEED:
5 large eggs
1 cup granulated sugar, sifted (250 ml; 210 g)
1 orange
1 lemon
¼ cup orange juice (60 ml)
2 tablespoons lemon juice (30 ml)
¾ cup matzoh meal, sifted (185 ml; 113 g)
½ cup potato flour, sifted (125 ml; 80 g)
½ teaspoon salt (2.5 m.)
½ cup vegetable oil (125 ml)

Ingredients:

(To make one 9″ [23 cm] tube cake)

5 large eggs
½ cup granulated sugar, sifted (125 ml; 105 g)

2. Turn oven on to 325° F (165° C). Separate eggs (see Basic Skills), placing whites in one large bowl and yolks in small bowl. Beat whites with electric mixer *or* eggbeater until they get foamy and hold soft peaks on the tip of the beater. Then sift in ½ cup sugar. Beat whites until they hold *stiff* peaks. To test this, turn beater motor off and hold beater upside down; peaks should stand upright on tips of beaters. Set bowl aside.

How To:

1. When a baked sponge cake is cooling, it must be hung upside down so that it remains light and fluffy. If left to cool upright, it would fall flat.

   Locate a bottle that is stable enough to support your upside-down tube pan around its neck (see sketch). Set bottle and ungreased pan aside.

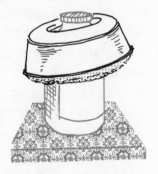

1 orange

1 lemon

¼ cup orange juice (60 ml)

2 tablespoons lemon juice (30 ml)

¾ cup matzoh meal, sifted (185 ml; 113 g)

½ cup potato flour, sifted (125 ml; 80 g)

½ cup granulated sugar, sifted (125 ml; 105 g)

½ teaspoon salt (2.5 ml)

½ cup vegetable oil (125 ml)

6. Pour *or* spoon batter into the ungreased tube pan. Batter will nearly fill pan, but don't worry, it will not rise enough during baking to spill over sides. Place pan in center of 350° F (175° C) oven and set timer for 50 to 60 minutes. Bake cake until cake tester *or* toothpick stuck in center comes out clean.

7. Use potholders to remove pan from oven. Still holding pan with potholders, immediately turn pan upside down over top of the bottle set aside in step 1. Be sure bottle is stable and won't tip over. Let cake hang this way until *absolutely cold*. Then set cake upright and loosen sides by sliding a knife between cake and pan sides. Set plate over cake top, hold both plate and pan together and flip them upside down, so plate is underneath. Tap pan bottom and cake should fall out. If it sticks, work knife gently between cake and pan sides again. The colder the cake, the easier it comes out of the pan.

3. Over a piece of wax paper, grate the peel (not the white inner layer) of the orange and lemon. Scoop up the peel and place it in the bowl with the yolks. Squeeze the juice of the orange and lemon, re-move pits, and measure amounts. Add more juice from extra fruit if needed. Place juice in yolk-peel bowl.

4. In the second large bowl, sift in matzoh meal, potato flour, sugar, and salt. Stir. Make a hole in the middle of these dry ingredients, then pour in the yolk-juice mixture, cleaning the small bowl with the rubber scraper. Add the oil. Beat mix-ture very well until blended.

5. Fold the matzoh meal-yolk-oil mixture into the stiffly beaten whites. To do this, spoon the meal-yolk mixture onto the whites a little at a time. Turn your spoon (*or* whisk *or* rub-ber scraper) over and upside down through the mixture. Stir gently or air will be forced out of the whites. To make cake light, keep as much air in whites as possible. Fold mix-ture until it is well blended to-gether; do this carefully, for meal-yolk mixture tends to stay lumpy at first.

Yom Ha'azmaut

Yom Ha'azmaut is Israeli Independence Day. It is celebrated on the fifth day of Iyar (April–May) and is a day of rejoicing for Jewish people throughout the world because it commemorates the end of the *Diaspora,* or wandering, and the creation of the legal Jewish homeland in Israel in May of 1948.

Picnics and outings are popular events on this day, and picnic-basket foods are traditional, just as they are on Lag B'Omer.

Lag B'Omer

Lag B'Omer, the time for spring picnics and outings, is observed on the eighteenth day of Iyar (April–May). The holiday recalls several events in Jewish history.

About eighteen centuries ago, when the Jews of the region of Palestine lived under harsh Roman rule, they revolted in an attempt to establish religious freedom and independence. The great scholar Rabbi Akiba led this rebellion. The officers and soldiers were largely Akiba's pupils. The foremost commander was his student Bar Kokhba. The war was severe and devastating; in its midst, a plague brought illness that killed many more of Akiba's men. On the thirty-third day of the *Omer* (the counting of the days between Passover and Shavuot) the plague stopped. Thus, this holiday celebrates this miracle and honors the student-soldiers. It is called the "Scholars' Holiday."

In this same period, Roman law forbade the teaching of the Jewish religion. This was, however, done secretly. One rabbi, Rabbi Shimon Bar Yohai, who was discovered, fled with his son to the hills and lived in a cave for twelve years. During this time, his loyal students would pretend to go on picnics in order to sneak visits to him. After the Roman Emperor Hadrian died, the rabbi and his son returned home, on the thirty-third day of the *Omer.*

Today, students in Israel take picnics to visit the grave of Bar Yohai in the village of Meron in northern Galilee.

Traditional Lag B'Omer foods are all things that can be carried in a picnic basket: sandwiches, Bagels,* cakes, and cookies. (See Categorical Foods Index.)

BAGELS

D or p

Bagel-making probably originated in seventeenth-century Vienna, when a certain coffee shop sold round stirrup-shaped rolls to honor the Polish king, who loved to ride horseback. Our word for bagel derives from the German word *bugel* (stirrup).

Everyone loves bagels, but few know that their special texture comes from the fact that the raised dough is boiled before it is baked. This recipe is not difficult to make, and the results are great.

EQUIPMENT:
3 small bowls
Measuring cups and spoons
Small saucepan
Wooden spoon
Large mixing bowl
Rubber scraper
Ruler
2 large flat trays *or* platters
2 cookie sheets *or* jelly roll pans
Wax paper
Dutch oven *or* other large pot
Timer
Slotted spoon
Pastry brush
Spatula

Wire rack
Serrated knife

FOODS YOU WILL NEED:
¼ cup plus 2 tablespoons margarine (90 ml)
1 package active dry yeast (¼ ounce; 7 g)
¼ cup lukewarm water (60 ml)
1 cup milk (250 ml) *or* water (for *pareve*)
1 tablespoon granulated sugar (15 ml)
1 teaspoon salt (5 ml)
1 egg
4 cups all-purpose flour (1 liter; 665 g)
2 tablespoons vegetable oil (30 ml)

Optional:
poppy seeds, sesame seeds, Kosher salt

Ingredients:

(To make 24 bagels)

1 *or* 2 tablespoons margarine
(15 *or* 30 ml)
1 package active dry yeast
(¼ ounce; 7 g)
¼ cup lukewarm water (60 ml)

1 cup milk (250 ml) *or* water (for
pareve)

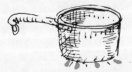

How To:

1. Grease cookie sheets *or* pans and set them aside.

2. In one small bowl, add yeast and warm *(not hot)* water. NOTE: Yeast is a living organism and hot temperatures will kill it. Set bowl aside until yeast softens and dissolves.

3. If using milk (which we think produces better results than water), measure it into a small saucepan and set it on the stove on medium heat just until little bubbles form around the edge of the milk's

¼ cup margarine, cut up in small bits (4 tablespoons; 60 ml)

1 tablespoon granulated sugar (15 ml)

1 teaspoon salt (5 ml)

1 egg

4 cups all-purpose flour (1 liter; 665 g)

1 tablespoon water (15 ml)

FOLD

PUSH

surface. Immediately remove milk from heat. Set pan on heat-proof surface and add margarine, sugar, and salt. Stir with wooden spoon. Set pan aside to cool to lukewarm. When lukewarm *(not hot)*, pour entire mixture into largest mixing bowl. Add dissolved yeast mixture and stir.

If using water for *pareve* bagels, run faucet until water is very hot. Measure hot water into largest mixing bowl. Add margarine, sugar, and salt. Stir, then set aside to cool to lukewarm. When no longer hot, stir in dissolved yeast mixture.

4. Separate egg (see Basic Skills) and put yolk in one small bowl *or* cup and white in another. Add 1 tablespoon (15 ml) water to yolk and beat well. Set bowls aside.

5. Wash your hands. Measure about 2 cups (500 ml) flour into large bowl over liquid-yeast mixture. Stir until well blended. Stir in egg *white*, then beat until combined with batter. Add remaining 2 cups flour (500 ml) a little at a time, beating between additions. When dough will hold a ball shape, turn it out onto a lightly floured board *or* work surface. Knead dough by folding it over toward you, then pushing it away while leaning on it with the heels of your hands. Give dough a quarter turn

and repeat. If dough feels sticky, add a little more flour. You may use more or less than the 4 cups of flour, depending upon how damp or how dry the weather is. Knead dough until it is shiny and smooth and no longer sticky to the touch.

6. Wash and dry mixing bowl. Grease bowl with 1 tablespoon (15 ml) oil, add dough ball, and turn it over to coat it with oil. Cover dough with a piece of oiled wax paper. Set bowl in warm (not hot) place until dough rises to double its size (about 1½ hours at 70° F [21° C]).

PUNCH!

7. When dough is risen, *punch*! it down to remove some of the air. Put dough on floured surface and knead it again for several minutes. Then divide dough into 4 equal pieces. Divide each piece into 6 equal balls.

8''

8. Sprinkle a little flour over 2 wax-paper covered trays *or* platters and set them aside. On floured work surface, roll each dough ball—one at a time—into a rope roughly ½" (1 cm) thick and 8" (20 cm) long. Form each rope into a ring with a 1" (2.5 cm) hole in the center. Fasten rope ends by spreading a drop or two of water on each end, then overlapping and pinching them together firmly. Ends will come apart when boiled if not well fastened. Set each dough ring on the floured

tray *or* platter. When all rings are made, cover trays with wax paper spread lightly with oil, and set them in warm (not hot) place for about 20 minutes.

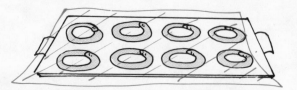

9. During this 20 minutes, fill a Dutch oven *or* pot about ½ full of water. Set pot on stove over high heat. Bring water to a boil. If water boils before 20 minutes are up, lower heat and keep water hot until ready to use.

10. Turn oven on to 400° F (205° C). Turn up heat under water to bring it back to a full boil. *Ask an adult to help with this step.* Carefully and gently lift dough rings off trays one at a time with your fingers. Set rings one at a time on slotted spoon and lower them into boiling water. Put 4 to 6 rings at a time into boiling water, depending on size of your pot. When bagels rise to surface of water, set timer for 5 minutes.

During the 5 minutes you boil each batch, you will see the dough puff up and the rings begin to look like real bagels. When the time is up, *ask an adult to help you* lift each ring from the water with the slotted spoon. Try to tip the spoon slightly to drain off water. Set boiled bagels directly on greased cookie sheet *or* jelly roll pan.

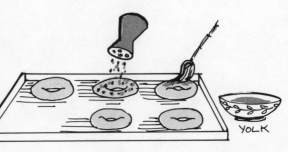

Immediately, brush top of each bagel with yolk mixture. Sprinkle tops with poppy seeds *or* sesame seeds *or* Kosher salt. At once, before bagels deflate, place baking sheet in preheated 400° F (205° C) oven and set timer for 20 minutes.

YOLK

11. Repeat step 10, boiling batches of bagels, glazing them with yolk and seeds, and adding them to oven as soon as they are ready. Bake each batch of bagels 20 to 35 minutes, or until bagel tops look golden-brown. Remove sheets from oven with potholders. Lift bagels with spatula and set to cool on wire racks.

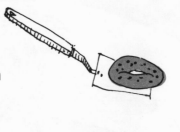

To serve, *ask an adult to help you* use serrated knife to cut bagel in half cross-wise. Serve toasted or cold, spread with cream cheese and lox *or* whitefish, *or* other favorite spread.

Shavuot

The sixth and seventh days of Sivan (May–June) mark the celebration of Shavuot, a religious as well as agricultural holiday. The origin of the festival dates from ancient times when, on the second day of Passover, farmers brought offerings of barley (*Omer*) to the temple. On this day, the counting of the weeks began; Shavuot, celebrating the wheat harvest, was observed on the fiftieth day after the bringing of the *Omer*. At the traditional Shavuot thanksgiving feast, a sheaf of wheat, two loaves made of new wheat flour, and new fruits of the harvest were offered to God. Thus, the holiday is also called the "Feast of First Fruits."

Shavuot also commemorates the day on which God gave Moses the Ten Commandments on Mount Sinai. Jewish homes are decorated with fruits and flowers; cakes, cookies, and fruit arrangements are sometimes designed in mountain (cone) shapes to resemble Mount Sinai.

In memory of the agricultural origin of the day, and to symbolize the "sweetness of the land and the Torah," favorite Shavuot foods are dairy dishes such as milk and honey, Blintzes,* Cheesecake,* Cream Sherbet,* and Noodle Pudding* made with cottage cheese and fruit.

GRANDPA HARRY'S EGGS AND TSIBELES   p or D

Tsibeles (tsi'-bu-les) means onions, and in this case they are simmered in water until very sweet, then cooked with scrambled eggs to make an unusual and delectable combination. My grandfather brought this recipe with him when, as a boy, he came to America from his home in Lodz, Poland. Whenever our whole family gathered, he would treat us to his breakfast specialty.

EQUIPMENT:
Cutting board and knife
Measuring cup and spoons
10″ (25.5 cm) frying pan
Mixing bowl
Eggbeater *or* whisk
Wooden spoon
Serving platter

FOODS YOU WILL NEED:
2 small onions
Cold water
Salt and pepper
4 medium *or* 3 large eggs
1 tablespoon margarine (for *pareve*) or butter (15 ml)

Ingredients:

(To serve 3 or 4; plan on 1 egg per person)

2 small onions
1 cup cold water (250 ml)
Salt and pepper
4 medium *or* 3 large eggs
1 generous tablespoon margarine (for *pareve*) *or* butter (15 ml)

How To:

1. On cutting board, chop onion into fine pieces (see Basic Skills). You should have about 1 cup (250 ml) of pieces. Place chopped onion in frying pan and add about a cup of cold water—just enough to cover onions. Add a pinch of salt and pepper. Set pan over medium heat until water is boiled out (about 10 minutes).

2. While onions are cooking, break eggs one at a time into measuring cup, pick out any shells, then add eggs to mixing bowl. Beat all eggs together well. Add a pinch of salt and pepper. Set eggs aside.

3. When water is boiled out, add margarine *or* butter to onions in frying pan. Stir while cooking over medium heat until onions turn a light golden color (about 2 minutes).

4. When onions are golden, pour the beaten eggs over them. Stir egg-onion mixture with wooden spoon and cook over medium heat as you would regular scrambled eggs. Cook and stir until mixture reaches desired doneness. Spoon mixture onto serving platter, add a little salt and pepper to taste and serve at once.

(85)

NANNY CLARA'S NOODLE PUDDING

All the traditional Shavuot "sweetness of the land" is contained in this one pudding, so rich is it in dairy products and fruits. Serve the pudding warm *or* cold, as a dessert, or as a side dish accompanied by meat *or* poultry. NOTE: This is an extra-large recipe because it is so popular there never seems to be enough; however, you can cut it in half to make less if you prefer.

EQUIPMENT:
Dutch oven *or* large pot with lid
Colander
Measuring cups and spoons
Vegetable peeler
Cutting board
Paring knife
Small mixing bowl
Eggbeater *or* large spoon
Baking dishes: 13½" × 8¾" × 1¾" (34 × 22 × 4.5 cm) lasagna-type pan *plus* one 8" (20 cm) pie pan
Timer
Potholders

FOODS YOU WILL NEED:
Large box broad egg noodles (12 ounces; 330 g); about 8 cups before cooking

5 to 6 tablespoons butter *or* margarine (90 ml)
3 medium-sized apples
4 eggs
5 tablespoons granulated sugar (75 ml)
¾ teaspoon salt (4 ml)
½ teaspoon cinnamon (2.5 ml)
½ teaspoon ground nutmeg (2.5 ml)
12-ounce carton cottage cheese 1⅔ cups; 400 g)
16-ounce carton sour cream (1⅔ cups; 425 g)
1 cup milk (250 ml)
1 cup golden *or* regular seedless raisins (250 ml; 160 g)
1 cup dried apricot halves (250 ml; 140 g)
⅓ cup toasted wheat germ (80 ml)

Ingredients:

(To make 12 to 14 servings)

Large box broad egg noodles (12 ounces; 330 g), about 8 cups before cooking

3 tablespoons butter *or* margarine (45 ml)

2 to 3 tablespoons butter *or* margarine (30 to 45 ml)

How To:

1. Follow directions on box to boil noodles in large pot of salted water until just tender. Set colander in sink. When noodles are cooked, *ask an adult to help you* carry pot to sink. Turn your head away to avoid steam and pour noodles into colander to drain off water. Return drained noodles to empty pot, stir in butter *or* margarine and set aside.

2. While noodles are cooking, grease baking pans well with butter *or* margarine.

3 medium-sized apples

4 eggs

5 tablespoons granulated sugar (75 ml)

¾ teaspoon salt (3.7 ml)

½ teaspoon cinnamon (2.5 ml)

½ teaspoon ground nutmeg (2.5 ml)

12-ounce carton cottage cheese (1⅔ cups; 400 g)

16-ounce carton sour cream (1⅔ cups; 425 g)

1 cup milk (250 ml)

1 cup golden *or* regular seedless raisins (250 ml; 160 g)

1 cup dried apricot halves (250 ml; 140 g)

⅓ cup toasted wheat germ (80 ml)

3. Turn oven on to 350° F (175° C). Peel apples with vegetable peeler. Use paring knife on cutting board to cut apples into slices about ¼" (0.5 cm) thick. Throw away cores. You should have about 2 cups (500 ml; 240 g) sliced apples. Add apple slices to buttered noodles in pot.

4. Break eggs one at a time into measuring cup, pick out shell bits, then add eggs to small bowl. Beat eggs with egg-beater *or* spoon.

5. To noodle-apple mixture in pot, add sugar, salt, cinnamon, nutmeg, cottage cheese, sour cream, milk, raisins, and beaten eggs from step 4.

   Cut apricots into small bits and add them to mixture as well. Stir all ingredients until well blended.

6. Spoon noodle mixture from pot into greased pans. The large pan holds about 8 cups mixture, the small pan about 4 cups (about 1 liter). Sprinkle wheat germ evenly over top of both pans. Set pans in 350° F (175° C) oven and set timer to bake 40 minutes, or until puddings are golden-brown on top. Remove from oven with potholders and set pans on heat-proof surface to cool. Serve warm *or* cold.

REBECCA GOLD'S BLINTZES

D

Blintzes, a thin, light pancake filled with cheese, is a traditional Shavuot recipe because it uses so many dairy products. Coming from my paternal grandmother, this recipe is of Romanian origin, although it is closely related to Russian *blini* and French *crêpes.*

EQUIPMENT:
2 large mixing bowls
Blender—optional
Measuring cups and spoons
Whisk *or* mixing spoon
6″ (15 cm) frying pan and 10″ to 12″
  (25.5 to 30.5 cm) frying pan
Wax paper
Large flat serving platter
Pancake turner

FOODS YOU WILL NEED:
5 eggs

⅔ to 1 cup water (160 to 250 ml)
1 teaspoon salt (5 ml)
1 cup all-purpose flour (250 ml; 165 g)
1 teaspoon vanilla extract (5 ml)
1 tablespoon granulated sugar (15 ml) plus
  extra for sprinkling over blintzes as topping
Pinch of cinnamon
1 pound pot cheese (450 g)
½ pound cottage cheese (200 g)
Margarine for frying
1 pint sour cream (550 g)—for topping
  blintzes

Ingredients:

(To make 14 to 16 blintzes)

4 eggs
⅔ to 1 cup water (160 to 250 ml)
1 teaspoon salt (5 ml)
1 cup all-purpose flour (250 ml;
  165 g)

1 egg
1 teaspoon vanilla extract (5 ml)
1 tablespoon granulated sugar
  (15 ml)
Pinch of cinnamon
1 pound pot cheese (450 g)
½ pound cottage cheese (200 g)

Margarine

How To:

To Make Blintzes Batter:

1. In mixing bowl *or* blender, combine eggs, ⅔ cup water, salt, and beat well. Add flour last while stirring with whisk. Beat well until the consistency of heavy cream. Add a little more water as needed to thin batter. Let stand until ready to use.

To Make Filling:

2. In second large mixing bowl, combine egg, vanilla, sugar, and cinnamon. Beat well with whisk *or* spoon. Add a little more sugar if you like, to taste. Then add both pot and cottage cheeses and stir well.

3. To fry blintzes, place about ½ tablespoon (7.5 ml) margarine in 6" (15 cm) frying pan. Set pan on stove over medium-high heat. Pan is hot enough when a drop of water sizzles when it hits the pan. Don't let margarine smoke or burn. Add about ¼ cup (60 ml) batter to hot pan. *Immediately*, lift pan and tilt it until batter covers bottom of pan in even layer. Pour any extra batter back into bowl.

   NOTE: Pan must be hot enough for batter to coat it evenly; batter must be thin enough to run smoothly over bottom of pan. Add a little more liquid to batter if it is too thick. You may need to fry several *test* blintzes before they will work perfectly.

4. After pan bottom is coated with batter, return pan to medium-high heat on stove. Cook 15 to 20 seconds, until edges of blintz start to curl, center looks dry, and bottom underside is a light golden color. *Cook on one side only.*

   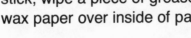

   Remove pan from stove, turn off heat, and turn pan upside down over a piece of wax paper set nearby. Sharply tap edge of upside down pan on table and blintz will drop out. Set it flat on the paper to cool. Repeat. If the blintzes start to stick, wipe a piece of greased wax paper over inside of pan.

5. To fill blintzes, set them flat, one at a time, with cooked side down. Put about 1½ tablespoons (22 ml) filling near bottom edge (a). Fold bottom edge over filling (b). Fold over sides (c), then hold sides as shown (d), with forefingers tucked into sides while rolling top edge down. Roll from top to bottom to complete the envelope. Set blintz on platter with open edge down.

   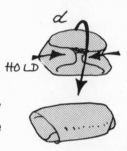

6. To cook filled blintzes, melt about 1 tablespoon (15 ml) margarine in large frying pan over medium heat. Depending upon pan size, you can fry 2 or 3 blintzes at a time. Use pancake turner to set filled blintzes down into pan with open edge down. Fry blintzes 35 to 45 seconds, until bottom is golden brown. Then turn blintzes over very carefully and fry on other side until golden-brown. Add more margarine and repeat, frying all blintzes. Place them on serving platter, open edge down, and serve warm; or chill them in refrigerator and serve them cold. Traditionally, blintzes (warm or cold) are served topped with a heaping tablespoon of sour cream. Sometimes this is topped with sprinkled sugar and/*or* cinnamon *or* fresh berries. Leftover blintzes—without sour cream—may be frozen.

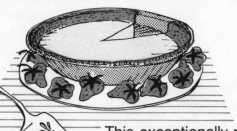

HAROLD'S CHEESECAKE

D

This exceptionally rich and delicious cake is filled with the dairy ingredients of Shavuot. It is easy to prepare because the ingredients are mixed in a blender.

EQUIPMENT:
Small saucepan
9″ (23 cm) pie plate
Large mixing bowl
Plastic bag
Rolling pin
Measuring cups and spoons
Fork
Electric blender (or electric mixer or mixing spoon)
Rubber scraper
Timer
Potholders

FOODS YOU WILL NEED:
6 tablespoons butter or margarine (90 ml)
1 cup graham cracker crumbs or 8 whole, double graham crackers (250 ml)
1 cup granulated sugar (250 ml; 210 g)
¼ teaspoon cinnamon (1.2 ml)
¼ teaspoon ground nutmeg (1.2 ml)
2 eggs
2 teaspoons vanilla extract (10 ml)
1½ cups sour cream (375 ml)
2 (8-ounce; 454 g) packages cream cheese, at room temperature

Ingredients:

(To make one 9″ pie [23 cm])

6 tablespoons butter or margarine (90 ml)

1 cup graham cracker crumbs or 8 whole, double, graham crackers (250 ml)
½ cup granulated sugar (125 ml; 105 g)
¼ teaspoon cinnamon (1.2 ml)
¼ teaspoon ground nutmeg (1.2 ml)

How To:

1. Turn oven on to 325° F (165° C).

2. Melt butter or margarine in small saucepan on low heat. Set aside until ready to use.

   To Make Crust:

3. Put whole crackers into plastic bag, twist top closed, set bag on counter and roll or beat with rolling pin until crackers are finely crushed. Measure out 1 cup of crumbs (250 ml) and place in bowl. Add sugar, cinnamon, and nutmeg. Measure and add 4 tablespoons (60 ml) of melted butter or margarine. (Save rest for later use). Mix ingredients together with a fork. Wash your hands.

4. Pour crumb mixture into pie plate. Use your hands *or* back of a spoon to press crumb mixture flat all over bottom and sides of plate. Set plate aside while making filling.

To Make Filling:

2 eggs
½ cup granulated sugar (125 ml; 105 g)
2 teaspoons vanilla extract (10 ml)
1½ cups sour cream (375 ml)
2 (8-ounce; 454 g) packages cream cheese, at room temperature

5. Add to container of blender (*or* bowl) eggs, sugar, vanilla, and sour cream. Cover blender and mix for about 20 seconds (*or* beat in bowl with beater or mixing spoon until well blended). Remove blender container from motor base. Lift lid and add cream cheese and remaining melted butter *or* margarine. Replace lid, set on motor, and blend another 20 seconds (*or* beat all ingredients in bowl until smooth).

6. Pour filling mixture into prepared pie plate. Use rubber scraper to clean out all filling. Place pie in 325° F (165° C) oven and set timer to bake 40 minutes. Remove pan from oven with potholders and set on heat-proof surface to cool. Then chill in refrigerator before serving. Filling may look soft after baking, but will firm up when cold.

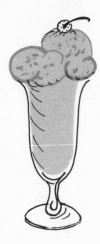

LEMON CREAM SHERBET

D

This rich cream sherbet is surprisingly easy to make—only two steps: blend and freeze. Depending on the fruit juice you use, you can flavor it with lemon, lime, *or* orange. It makes an elegant dessert, one you might enjoy preparing for a family dinner *or* serving in cones for your friends at a party.

EQUIPMENT:
Measuring cups and spoons
Electric blender *or* mixer
1-quart (or larger) freezer container
Rubber scraper

FOODS YOU WILL NEED:
1 pint heavy whipping cream (500 ml)
¼ cup sour cream *or* plain yogurt (60 ml)
1 (6-ounce) can frozen lemonade concentrate (no water added) (178 ml)
⅔ cup granulated sugar (160 ml; 150 g)
¼ teaspoon salt (1.2 ml)
Grated rind of 2 lemons (about 3 tablespoons, 45 ml)

Ingredients:

(To make about 1 quart sherbet [0.5 liter], 8 servings)

1 pint heavy whipping cream (500 ml)
¼ cup sour cream *or* plain yogurt (60 ml)
1 (6-ounce) can frozen lemonade concentrate (no water added)
⅔ cup granulated sugar (160 ml; 150 g)
¼ teaspoon salt (1.2 ml)
Grated rind of 2 lemons (about 3 tablespoons; 45 ml)

How To:

---

1. Measure all ingredients into blender container *or* bowl. Blend (covered) *or* beat about 2 minutes, or until thick and smooth.

2. Pour mixture into freezer container, emptying blender *or* bowl with rubber scraper. Freeze several hours or overnight until hard. Remove from freezer about 20 minutes before serving so it will not be too hard. NOTE: To vary flavor, you can use different juice concentrates as well as grated orange *or* lime rind.

Categorical Foods Index

Alphabetical Index